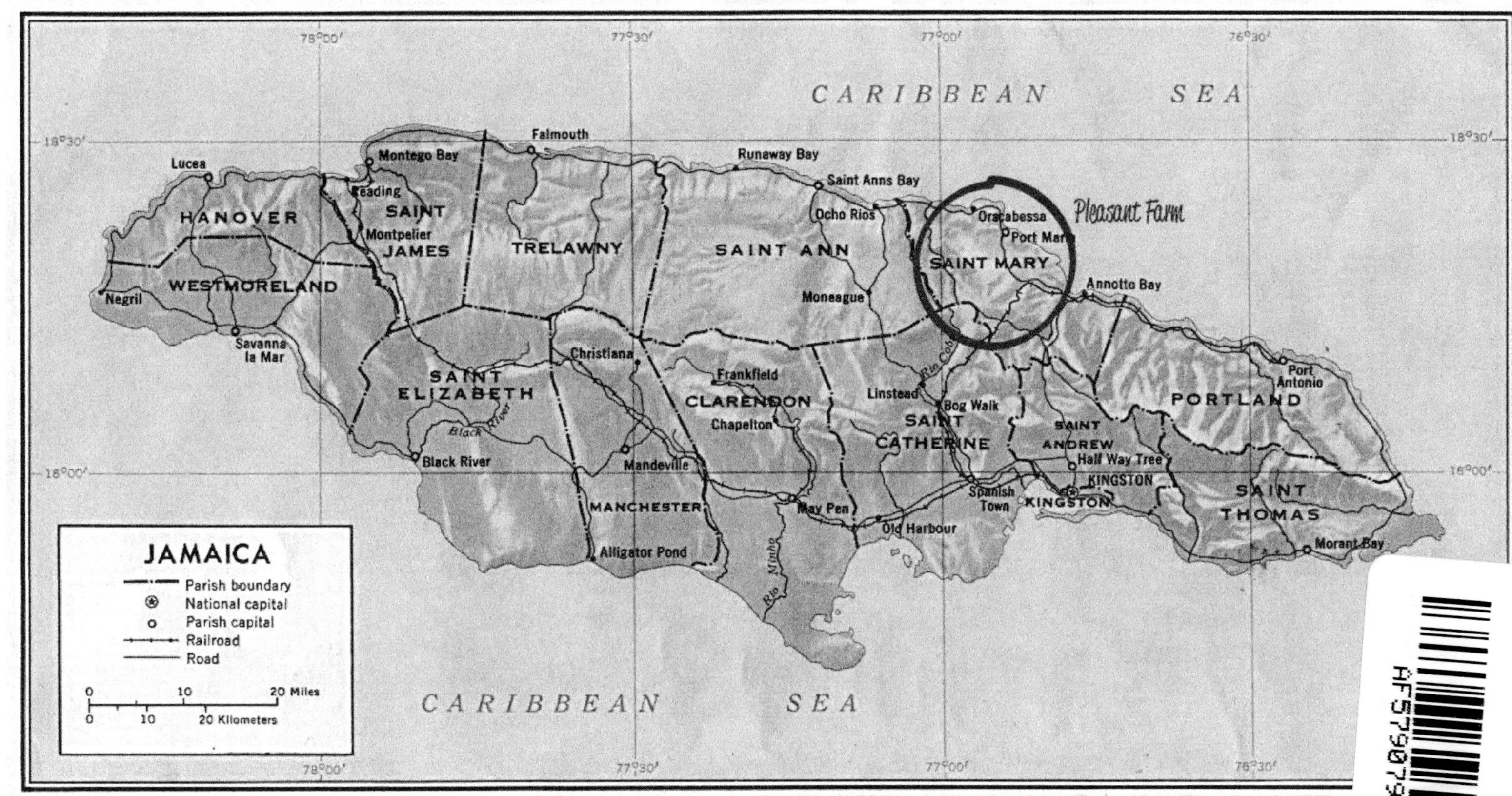
JAMAICA
Parish boundary
National capital
Parish capital
Railroad
Road
0 10 20 Miles
0 10 20 Kilometers
CARIBBEAN SEA
CARIBBEAN SEA
Pleasant Farm
HANOVER
WESTMORELAND
SAINT JAMES
TRELAWNY
SAINT ANN
SAINT MARY
PORTLAND
SAINT ELIZABETH
MANCHESTER
CLARENDON
SAINT CATHERINE
SAINT ANDREW
SAINT THOMAS
Lucea
Negril
Savanna la Mar
Montego Bay
Montpelier
Falmouth
Runaway Bay
Saint Anns Bay
Ocho Rios
Moneague
Oracabessa
Annotto Bay
Port Antonio
Christiana
Frankfield
Linstead
Bog Walk
Chapelton
Black River
Mandeville
Alligator Pond
May Pen
Old Harbour
Spanish Town
Half Way Tree
KINGSTON
Morant Bay
Rio Cobre
Rio Minho
Black River
78°00′
77°30′
77°00′
76°30′
18°30′
18°00′

6/2021

To Bev Wight with love & thanks

A Jamaican Dawn

... in this post-pandemic Dawn!

Beverly Ramsay

Acknowledgements

I wish to thank my many readers including those in schools, libraries and the many institutions and clubs who gave me a platform to promote my first book 'A Jamaican Childhood'. Through your valued support I have felt empowered to write this second volume of stories.

I also wish to thank my family and friends at home, and abroad (USA, Canada and beyond) who, during the pandemic and lockdown, encouraged me to continue writing. I feel certain that they will enjoy the fruits of their encouragement.

Last but not least, I wish to thank my fabulous illustrator Sarah Dixon, who I can safely say is without compare at capturing the essence of my books and conveying it, in all its vibrant glory, on to the cover of each publication.

Biography

Beverly Ramsay was born in the parish of St.Ann, Jamaica.

Before her parents left for England in the latter part of the 1950s, she went to live with her maternal grandparents at Pleasant Farm in the district of Retreat, St. Mary. Then one year after Jamaican Independence, she left her rural life to join her parents in London.

On leaving school, she attended Goldsmiths College, University of London where she qualified as a teacher before taking up her first teaching post in Brixton; the area in which she had lived with her family on her arrival from Jamaica.

As well as documenting her experiences at Pleasant Farm in 'A Jamaican Childhood' and in her latest book 'A Caribbean Dawn', she also produces a wide variety of multicultural teaching materials.

Introduction

Through these evocative recollections of Cassie in 'A Jamaican Dawn', we are transported back in time to the 1950s through stories which are full of humour, surprises and even horror.

As we follow the intrepid little girl through the lush Jamaican landscape in and around Pleasant Farm, we meet amazing characters, discover new cultural practices and make jaw-dropping discoveries from morning to night, over many weeks, months, and even years.

Through the rich and lyrical language of 'A Jamaican Dawn' our narrator recreates for the reader, memorable events and sights and sounds so vivid, that they might even reawaken the reader's own childhood memories.

We hope you will enjoy this extra delicious slice of childhood memories. They were baked specially for you!

ISBN 9798566847689

Contents

Daybreak

Dawn, when it broke in all its magnificence over Pleasant Farm, Jamaica, British West Indies, did so in its usual dramatic and flamboyant fashion. Did so with style, as only nature can when it chooses to display its magnificent creations under its ultimate light source – the sun.

It is only six in the morning, and already the fierce sunlight has burst impatiently through a blindingly blue and cloudless sky. And now, not content to just sit quietly hovering and shimmering on the blazing horizon, it extends its never-ending rays beyond all it surveys, and barges uninvited into the sleeping places of creatures far and wide, quickly making its way under all available doors too, and right into the abodes of humans. And like a silent alarm clock, it creeps through one pair of gently fluttering cotton curtains and into the semi-darkness of the room which contains the sleeping child.

This is where the little girl, Cassandra – better known as Cassie, lies; still sleeping and dreaming of running through fields of languidly waving yellow corn while she pauses to sniff and pick the surrounding wildflowers as she goes. The golden rays find her, and feeling their gentle warmth, she slowly awakens to the clear yellow brightness which highlights the sheen of her nut-brown skin.

Then while peeping through splayed fingers which act as soft filters, she dreamily basks in the glow before the sudden scream of the lone cockerel jolts her into full consciousness. She knows exactly where he is! Yes, she pictures him perched majestically as usual on his not too distant fence as he heralds all, far and wide, with his raucous and repetitive cook-a-doodle-doos.

He, this breaker of sleep and dreams is the well-known and

flamboyant yellow, red, gold, and brown-feathered bird now standing drowned in morning sunlight. He literally rules the roost. And were it not a known fact to the two adult owners of this swathe of green and fecund piece of real-estate, that his contribution to the continuation of their chicken livestock and the never ending production of white and darkly speckled eggs was so dependent on the noisy creature, his reign in a land whose national dish is chicken, would have been brutally cut short a long time ago. Either some say from a hastily thrown shoe, or a well-aimed rock-stone. And once, after too many delicious sleeps had been interrupted, Mrs.O.Walker, that usually gracious lady, wife to the debonair Mr S Walker and grandmother to Cassie, had voiced her opinion that he would have made a nice main course for a lovely Sunday dinner, along with the usual accompaniment of rice and freshly picked peas and salad. All washed down nicely with a big glass of sorrel swirling tantalisingly with slices of lime and cubes of ice, before they retired for their customary Sunday afternoon nap.

But now, his continued repetitive early morning wake-up call suggested that he knew only too well of his invincibility. And many a times after the good lady had been dragged reluctantly into wakefulness she had been heard to say resignedly with an accompanying tutting of her tongue 'Lawd help us! It's dat damn cock tearing out his throat at such an unearthly hour of the day again!' And she had rolled over, shielding her eyes from the rising yellow glow as she prepared for another snooze.

The raucous caterwauling of the cockerel eventually subsides, with the last note seeming to be comprised of only a breathless 'do', before the space is filled by the staccato type barking of numerous dogs. Their competitive sounding ru-ru-ruffing forms the main base soundtrack to the rising cacophonous singing and squawking of various species of birds. Some of these background singers are on the wing and are visible while others are very carefully camouflaged by the variegated foliage of the large surrounding trees in which they sit consuming fruits or insects or both.

But back inside the sleeping house, Cassie, awake and listening, is trying hard to resist the morning reveille. But not able to maintain her position for long, she rises in one smooth leap, abandons the warm cocoon of her much loved wheeled Vono-Vee bed and absently wipes the back of one hand across her sleepy eyes as she makes her way towards the window. Then lifting the fluttering curtains, she peers out onto her surroundings while using one hand as a visor against the blinding rays of the rising sun.

And yes! There it is. Lying in all its splendour before her and around her, like a huge spherical glass paperweight, displaying all its variations of greens and blues as far as the eye can see. All is decorated by huge splashes of colours which seem to be taken from a newly opened box of water-colour paints of such finely variegated hues that the colours seem to merge and intermingle into one. It is a pallet created by an enormous landscape of flowers, blossoms, and fruits of such variety that their mingling is seamless as they reach longingly towards the clear blue sky above.

And the child, her chin resting languidly on folded arms, which are in turn supported by the broad sill of the window, silently surveys the land with amazement and wonder as her eyes travel back and forth over the scene like a camera, recording the undulations of the terrain which is unfolding like new, around her. She smiles and reminds herself that the land she surveys in every direction is her very own playground. And that it is all waiting to be explored. Right now!

So still in her nightclothes and what her grandparents laughingly refers to as her 'English bedroom slippers', she rushes out of the rising heat of the house, leaps over the steps designed for just such a purpose, and embraces the fresh morning air. And with her nightdress softly billowing out behind her, she flings her arms upwards in wild abandonment, and after performing her trademark twirl while still walking, her feet begin to gather momentum and she begins the first leg of her journey.

Her first visit is to the large chicken coop where she carefully inspects the glossy hen and her busy brood. The softly clucking mother looks at her with what the small child construes to be a friendly smile and the look does not fail to remind her of how she became the owner of this beloved pet, now clothed in glossy brown feathers. She had been an unhatched and abandoned chick – one of a clutch of eight round and freckled brown eggs, but so determined was the still encased creature to join her hatched siblings that she had sent out weak desperate cheeps from inside the unbroken shell. And the child being closer to the ground and with sharper hearing than her grandmother, had detected amongst the sea of happy cheeping and motherly clucking, the desperate cry of the unhatched chick. And she had insisted with tearful pleas on its immediate release.

So, to abate her distress, the cheeping egg had been gently cracked and the small wet and egg-shaped creature duly released and then placed into the warm and quivering, outstretched palms of the entranced little girl. The gift became her responsibility and she had happily and often in a spellbound state, observed each passing phase of her chicken. From its ability to stand and then to run, to the thickening of its yellow feathers, the changing of its beak, and then its transformation into a beautiful golden-brown, glossy-feathered strutting hen.

And often the pair, child and chick, along with some accompanying dogs were to be seen roaming the outskirts of the farm and even on the nearby street, where they created much mirth for the local population. And it was on one of those days, after their usual walk that her grandmother had announced without any further embellishments, that her hen would be laying an egg any day now. The news was accepted with glee. There was however, one aspect of the pronouncement which baffled her. And so unable to contain her curiosity as to how the egg had been created, she crossed what instinct warned her might be a dangerous boundary for a Jamaican child. Nevertheless, a small voice, foreign and not familiar with the strictures of the culture, urged her on to enquire.

So, turning her face upwards and looking straight into the serious face of her grandmother, she revealed her curiosity on issues connected with procreation and asked the supremely innocent words of 'How do you know, grandma?' But the lady's granite-like expression which looked down at her, caused her small voice of courage and curiosity to melt away. And during the heavy silence which ensued, the matriarch rose hurriedly and without a word, bustled off in a very business-like manner, her flower-strewn dress swishing from side to side to indicate that the subject was closed. And the child now wreathed in bafflement, looked in her mind's eye, and saw not one, two or three or even four eggs, but a whole clutch of six, all brown and heavily freckled, lying tantalisingly in a nest – just like the ones she'd seen right there on the farm and in many of her reading books. Then sure enough as predicted by the matriarch, there was an egg and then a whole clutch of them which had in turn, resulted in the present scene.

And now on bended knees she greets her hen and gently lifts her wings to stare at the soft yellow chicks as if seeing them for the very first time. Then silently and almost reverentially, she watches with delight as they with no apparent sense of direction, stumble haphazardly over each other in their search for something neither they nor the little girl is ever able to find. And in her belief that the hen understands her language, she reports to what she feels is the listening face of her pet, saying in a serious tone, 'Yes they are all here. Yes, all six of them'. And in turn, the attentive and trusting face of the mother hen looks back at her with her slow-blinking gimlet eyes, just like a solicitous grown-up would. Then happy with the results of her observations and of her successful communication, the child, as she has done since the hatching, rearranges each of the hen's ruffled feathers before she bids the family a temporary goodbye. And as the child takes her leave, the hen sweeps her roving eyes in all directions, while her face reverts to the alert watchfulness of a mother.

Treading purposefully across the lush green lawn, Cassie is as always, entranced and mesmerised by the delicate dew which lies sparkling on the leaves, the flowers and on every single blade of grass. She closely inspects the delicate globules of water which lies on the petals of one flower and notes in awe, that each water-filled sac resembles a glittering jewel and that inside each one lies a minute and slightly oily-looking rainbow. She is also aware of the almost indiscernible trembling of the globules, and even though she has never seen a troupe of ballerinas performing a pas de deux for their audience, she holds on to the image and draws the comparison when much much later she observes the movements of such a troupe of dancers in a far off land. But she resists the urge to touch the outer casing of the water sacs, knowing they will disintegrate with what she imagines would be a silent pop. After which, some of their moisture would then be quickly drawn upwards by the heat, while tiny splashes would rush downwards and disappear forever, back into the warming earth.

But today, curiosity and the temptation to explore, to experiment, to discover, is overwhelming, and so her curious finger is unfurled. And it touches and pokes. And the sac burst with what she imagines is that expected but soundless, 'pop'! But there is no splintering of pictures or of the colourful rainbows. There is just water. Just like there had been in the last experiment and the one before that. Clear transparent water which coalesces and converges as it rushes swiftly along the central channel of the leaves and along the contours of the petals, gathering speed as it goes and before it crashes soundlessly into the thirsty earth.

Now she is standing directly under the canopy of the cherry tree, amongst which there are nests of various designs and sizes interspersed within the branches. And like a true country child she acknowledges the golden rule of not to disturb them but is still able to visualise, to imagine that inside each one of the intricately woven twig baskets, are eggs laid by a variety of birds. And all are painted in different shades from white to clotted cream, and sometimes even a vivid blue; and many are further decorated with brown spots and splodges of varying sizes. She knows that they are delicate and precious, so with the rule uppermost in her mind, she turns her attention instead to closely inspecting the progress of the tree and to look for signs and evidence of the long-awaited fruits.

Because she is a child and lacks the understanding of pollination, and also because everything around her is forever growing and blooming and bursting with life, she is bemused and confused by the same answer she receives to her constant questionings concerning the cherry tree. When will the cherry tree grow cherries? This she asks numerous times per week, and sometimes per day. And the unenlightening answer is always that there is a season for the cherry tree. And in response she will ask 'What is a season? Quickly followed by 'When will it arrive?' And although sometimes she receives a substantial answer, usually from her grandfather the part-time botanist, it is too complex and carries no logic or imagery so is not retained by the child. Because in a country where the sun is always shining, and there is no demarcation in time, temperature, or seasons, explanations have proved to be fruitless. So each day she revisits the tree in a bid to catch 'the season' of the cherry tree.

But today she is rewarded with buds! Magnificent in their profusion of pink lace-like furls slightly bursting through their tight jackets, their tips seeming to have been beautifully hand-rolled by expert fingers. These living pieces of fretwork lace lie in profusion on every branch, waiting to explode as they do each year, in their silent fanfare of release and escape from their dormant coiled-up state. Here they sit looking like a huge vase of blazing colour just past the corner of the L-shaped drive, ready to provide a welcome to all onlookers – residents and visitors alike. And it is that explosion of colour which she knows heralds the beginning of the long-awaited fruits.

Having lived at the farm since the age of four, she has learned over time that the season of the cherries is short, so she prepares herself for the battle that will ensue. The battle with the birds. And they seem to know, maybe better than she does, of when the season starts. They will, over the coming days and weeks be making short noisy visits to watch the progress of the tree. Just like her, they too will see the blossoms fall in profusion at the foot of the tree and feel the gentle breeze which will blow the petals clean away and onto the ground. And with their gimlet eyes they will hungrily watch the growth of the tiny green cherries as they develop at the end of the stem which gradually lengthens day by day to accommodate the increasing size of the longed-for delicacy.

And like the watching birds, the vigilant child will also note the gradual development of colour, like under a photographer's wash, from pale green to pink and then finally into their blazing show-stopping shiny red. The final state of perfection for which all the watchers wait. Then over the coming days and weeks as nature individually paints each maturing fruit, the battle will commence, and all the birds, like coloured rain, will descend from distant trees and from distant farms, and take their fill. As will the vigilant child who, seeing the tree as a part of her fiefdom will each day assert her right to partake of her portion from the fecund tree. So, on small legs rotating like ferris wheels in motion she will move with determination towards the tree while announcing excitedly over her shoulders to her amused grandparents, 'The cherries are ready grandma! Grandad!'.

And they will watch with delight as she takes her stance, not beside the tree but directly under its heavy and pendulous boughs, and along with some birds – those bold enough to remain in her presence – pick and eat, and peck, and gobble with a desperation not seen at any other time. And in her half-hidden state, her legs quite static, were once assumed to be trunks of the said tree by a short-sighted visitor. Then after her feasting, she loads a portion of the said fruits into the lap of her dress and takes them home. She knows that soon the birds with their voracious appetites, will pick the tree clean of its abundant bounty and all that will remain will be the leaves interspersed with dangling stalks - some still holding on to their picked-bare seeds which will lie suspended under the bleaching heat of the midday sun. And there will be scant evidence that the tree had once been a sea of red.

Next, she journeys towards the cool banana-walk where the tall majestic plants in their solid mass sits, while slowly producing the food which supports a great deal of the wealth of the farm. Today she notes the increasing growth of the bunch of baby bananas which hang from beneath the leafy head of each tree. And although counting them is an enjoyable pastime what fascinates her – but makes her shiver – is the strange green and red central appendage around which the hands of fruits are arranged, and which to her wild imagination resembles the tail of a bad creature mentioned in the Bible.

She knows from conversations that most of these bananas are destined for something referred to as export, that a portion will be eaten by birds even while they sit on the tree, and that some will also be eaten by her and the people who work on the farm, while those deemed overripe are destined for her grandmother's kitchen. Some of these will be made into cakes, while others, dark and very soft in their ripeness are destined to be stored with additional ingredients into rarely seen air-tight containers for long periods of time where, she is told but has never had any proof, they will slowly and miraculously be transformed into vinegar...

Then as the sun rose higher in the sky and leaves the dawn behind, Cassie quickly makes her way to the orange groves. Here she remembers how not so long ago the branches of each tree had borne only small buds, which now having opened, display their white flamboyant lace-like blossoms, delicately fringed with pink. She revels anew in the transformation of their size, their frothiness, their colour and of course their fragrance which she gulps in with glee. She hears the heavy murmuring of the bees and watches how the fat little creatures crawl like drunken people dressed in yellow and black striped shirts - in out and over the intoxicating florets, all the while humming and mimicking what sounds to her like the distant drone of traffic as they work to produce the next batch of delicious oranges – and delicious honey. And as she watches she is reminded of her aunt the bride , who, wearing a white lace wedding dress stiffened by three wide crinolines, had travelled along the very drive behind her, accompanied by her six little bridesmaids – one of which was Cassie – themselves dressed in frothy balls of pink satin and lace, just like the scene in front of which she now stands.

She is just about to plunge her face into a handful of delicious smelling blossoms when she recalls her grandmother's warning cry of 'Chile stap sticking your face in the blossoms before bees sting yu or you breathe one up into your nose. Don't let me have to write to yu parents in England and tell dem anyting happen to yu!' So, acknowledging the imagined words, she pauses and cast her mind to a day in the future when she will arrive and discover the beginnings of the longed for fruits; before they burst forth from their protective green foliage and flaunt themselves like shiny orange-coloured jewels.

With the heat rapidly rising, the child picks up her pace and skips towards the ever abundantly laden avocado tree where up to ten large green and shiny fruits lie around its base way below its leafy canopy. Sometimes some bear the scars on their leathery skin of having fallen from a great height, and reveal through the gash, the rich yellow and green-tinged fruit which rapidly turns grey as if in a bid to match the colour of the large round seed nestling inside. But today there are no casualties and the whole collection lie perfectly camouflaged in the long dew-sprinkled grass, as though waiting to be collected once more by her. She piles as many as she can into the skirt of her nightdress, before happily making her way home.

Up the short flight of broad steps she travels with her bounty into the doorless veranda and across the cool red terracotta tiles, into the large and dusky living room where she walks on the outside edge of the thick central rug which houses the large mahogany claw foot table, and finally into the dining room which is now bathed in sunlight filtering through the white lace curtains. The hum of the giant refrigerator greets her, and now feeling like the Elves visiting the house of the Shoemaker, she deposits her gifts into the waiting fruit bowl and places a stalk of her favourite flower into the ever present vase which sits half full, in the centre of the shiny mahogany dining table.

Her dawn tasks completed, she retraces her steps to the

adjoining room, takes a right turn and enters the silence of her bedroom where she removes her dew-soaked bedroom slippers, before slipping back into her still warm bed. And in the quiet yellow glow of her room, she lies waiting for her usual wakeup call while reflecting with delight on the transformations she has observed on her daily magical dawn walk.

Rainman From England

News of the impending visit of an overseas speaker was received with the usual levels of jubilation by the pupils of Flaxman All Age School.

Such exciting news not only offered them a reduction in the length of the school day, but released them during the visit from being under the too-close scrutiny of over-enthusiastic teachers or discipline during assembly. In addition to those benefits, the overseas visitors as opposed to the home-grown variety, promised a richer tapestry of news, ideas and on most occasions, surprises.

On receipt of the news, the children, like their peers all over the world, expressed their joy by giving a gentle jab of excitement to those closest to them in the assembled crowd. And of course, the most suitable time for this to take place was while the gaze of the head teacher or head boy had temporarily strayed in its heat-seeking ways towards other less circumspect recalcitrants, in the opposite direction – to the people who demanded their most urgent but unwanted attention.

Many of the children while quietly facing the front and without any change in their facial expressions, recalled the interminable boredom that had on many occasions been generated by the meandering recollections of pompous and patronising homegrown speakers. And they recalled with annoyance that almost all of that cohort while delivering their inconsequential bits of drivel, did so in faux American accents, the quality of which was judged in the words of their equally disgusted parents as 'A bruk up dere gums trying to speak the Queen's English'. So feeling grateful at escaping that breed of speakers, they basked under the warm rays of the sun and sent up a silent prayer of thanks while they reflected on past visitors who had travelled from distant shores and brought with them ideas and stories which caused them first to gasp and then to dream.

Always, their stories were rich with interesting landscapes and abounded with unexpected people creating and participating in incredible events and practices. Stories which caused the thirsty imaginations of the children to skip, hop and somersault wildly and freely as they were led on magical mystery tours beyond the boundaries of their classrooms, their homes, and their country. And at the culmination of these talks it could be assumed that every child in the audience would take away for a day, and sometimes maybe forever, vivid imagery, new words, and most important of all, lessons that would affect their perceptions of people, of the world and how to operate within it. And in addition to the life lessons, often delivered in new and interesting accents, it was their sartorial elegance which impressed the children. Often dressed as if preparing for a wedding, they felt honoured to know that they were worth dressing up for and in return gave these visitor great allowances to sermonise and moralise to them.

So to prepare for their visitor, much free time was given up to attend to the beautification of their school. A group of girls were deemed the Inside team, while the boys were consigned to the exterior. And each group, happy at being chosen from among numerous other willing applicants, set about their tasks with relish.

For the girls, this meant searching for, finding and scrubbing to death with lashings of eye-wateringly strong disinfectant, in conjunction with fistful of abrasive materials, layers upon layers of debris ingrained into the lids of wooden desks. And with some of these pieces being ancient, some almost dissolved under not only the strength of potent liquids but the onslaught of fiercely vigorous and enthusiastic young limbs. Quickly obliterated were numerous ink splashes, and some very ancient and deeply scratched drawings of love hearts and arrows – one of which faintly declared inside a heart that 'Astley loves Gertrude' – no doubt the names of a long-married pair – along with other similar and stubborn declarations.

Also found and demolished, were hidden items of sticky sweets, numerous grey non-identifiable globules, and some very tenacious pieces of chewing gums in various colours – 'From America of course' the children said. And many of these pieces, now rock hard, still bore the indentations of large teeth and told the story of being hastily extracted from vigorous jaws on the sudden appearance of a hawk-eyed teacher.

Then after all the nooks and crannies had been searched and violently scrubbed, and the wood made good as new with lashings of polish, the precious books were next on the agenda. Those that were positively dog-eared – not through malice or mistreatment of course – but from regular usage, were now glanced at or flicked though with fondness, dusted , and then had their frayed edges turned towards the back of the shelves where one of the cleaning team noted that they resembled sulky children standing in a corner with their faces firmly to the wall.

And while all this frenzy of fixing and cleaning and polishing, and talking and laughing took place inside, the other team was simultaneously engaged in beautifying the exterior of the long schoolhouse. It was a building that one of their interesting

English visitors had told them years before, had probably been modelled on houses found in a place called Suffolk which was situated deep in the English countryside. A place he said in many ways looked remarkably like this part of Jamaica. He had gone on to explain that a Suffolk Longhouse was a building where someone could walk from one room at the start, through countless adjoining doors into other rooms before the walker reached the final room at the far end of the building. And so, he had described the exact copy of the children's school, even down to the pink exterior often sported by such houses.

On the exterior of this Longhouse as it was thereafter referred to with a chuckle by many, the team who had billed themselves as the 'Outsiders' worked lovingly and diligently on all aspect of the structure. They too searched painstakingly to find and obliterate all marks and embellishment - many of which (secreted away in obscure corners) they laughingly noted, included declarations of hatred for a particular teacher, or less well-hidden professions of the love of one pupil for another. These included motifs such as 'Raymond loves Merna', and 'Creaton loves Val' and other such heartfelt declarations, all of which included the attendant embellishments of hearts, numerous kisses, and winged arrows. Then it was onto dousing the long line of windows with buckets of water before each individual pane was brought to its optimum state of transparency through the use of crumpled newspaper, copious amounts of hot breath, and the enthusiastic circular exercising of young arms. All of course accompanied by bouts of laughter and back-slapping.

Then on to the final job. One which they all agreed would produce the picture and ambience that they wished to present to their visitor – the trimming and beautifying of the lawn, driveway, and surrounding flowerbeds. Here they worked in pairs as instructed, and happily set about uprooting and obliterating anything that looked remotely like an unattractive weed. But a later inspection carried out by the headteacher revealed that much of what lay in the piles of rubbish were in fact rare specimens of plants that he had personally propagated and lifted from his own well stocked borders and transported to the school garden. To defuse the suppressed anger of the headteacher, one well-meaning boy had responded under inquisition with 'They never had any flowers on them sir!' which only brought him a withering look from the former. Then following the raking of the glistening white gravel driveway, the tired but satisfied children had finally engaged in devouring a substantial feast of hardough bread, bun, bulla cake and Jamaican cheese, all rounded off with lemonade laced with freshly squeezed lemons and chunks of cooling ice.

Finally, the longed-for day arrived. And with it being a special occasion, the headteacher was found not on the top step waiting for late comers and armed with a cane moving to and fro like a dangerous snake behind him, but standing at the entrance to the school, looking as though he had not left his post overnight. Filing past him and following their perfunctory greeting of 'Good morning sir' the children congregated at a distance in small huddles under the cool of the voluminous branches of the almond tree where they exchanged their thoughts and presumptions about their expected visitor. And as was the custom on these occasions, they also surveyed each other's sartorial and tonsorial displays, and without prior invitations, gave liberally to each other, their honest and sometimes playful but brutal opinions.

And so, it would begin.

"A like your uniform."

"Tanks"

'Yu pleat sharp, eeh?' someone would say admiringly

And in reply the answer came 'Yes me madda mek it for me last night'. And after a pause 'but a had to stay up late so she could fit it on me'.

And in another group someone would venture with a small chuckle while surveying the trousers of his peer, 'your crease look like knife eeh?' at which loud guffaws and backslappings were interspersed with utterances regarding how they had achieved their creases in their own trousers.

One boy volunteered that 'My fada do mine last night.' And added 'Yu should see how happy he was making dat crease wid my Granmadda's big ole heavy iron!'

And his audience, some with similar experiences, waited for the next episode. So, fulfilling their need for a story, he continued 'when him finish you should have seen im a slap his chest and a dance round the room like him mad. We laugh you si!' he added, laughing at the recollection. And his audience being aware of where they were, laughed quietly along with him while allowing their rocking bodies to soak up the mirth that could not be released from their mouths in the presence of the headteacher.

And among this and other groups too, there were some who had not been so careful with their own creases and hoped that the evidence would be ignored and passed over. But today of all days, there was no such luck. So with a large dose of derision in their voice, a bold person would ask point blank 'How your trousers crease look so dead bwoy?' before tempering his boldness in a softer tone for fear of being labelled a bully "Yu get up too late?'

'Yes' came a muttered response from the one under inspection before the anticipated mirthful cry of 'Wuthlis boy!' was fired back, accompanied by the obligatory bout of friendly laughter and gentle commiserating back-slapping.

Next on their agenda came hair - especially regarding styles and embellishments. Artificially straightened hair received the first comments.

'A didn't know yu hair so long!' someone would say, their voice full of surprise and admiration, while their fingers reached out aching to assess the length and texture of the admired plaits. And in the interim silence the same speaker would continue with a question 'Yu straighten it las night?'

And displaying genuine surprise followed by bemusement, the owner of the new style would answer 'Yu mad? For it to sweat out?'

Then a brave admirer in the crowd would, thinking herself unnoticed, extend tentative fingers to stroke the texture of the newly coiffured hair, before quickly withdrawing them as the owner seemingly acting on a sixth sense, visibly flinched away from the contact before issuing the universal warning always spoken – always in a semi-friendly tone – 'No man, don't touch mi hair! Yu mad?' And the expected ripple of nervous laughter would rise and die away.

Next on the agenda were shoes. Because in a land where not everyone had the good fortune to wear a pair to school, it was a touchy subject. The unwritten rule was that common sense should be exercised and discussions on the subject while in the company of those who had none, was strictly forbidden: Unless that is, someone really wanted to visit the headmaster in his office.

But there was relief in everyone's eyes because today, all were shod. And although some were of a delicate nature and not designed for a rough and tumble school day, the wearer seemed satisfied with their appearance. But it was also silently noted with sadness that there were absences amongst them. And many concluded, and rightly so, that the absences were due to the lack of footwear; And so they sympathised as they knew how their absent friends had dreamt and thirsted after this day and all that it promised. And an emotion which they could not name, stirred inside them and temporarily took their joy away. And many years later they were reminded of that moment, and of the supposed deprivations, and now with families of their own, they strived against disadvantages which they felt might blight their own children's future. And many found all those years later , that it was only through travelling to the land from where the visitor had come, that their dreams of a better life for their families could be achieved.

The ringing of the school bell ended their inspections and alerted them that the hour had arrived. And the army of blue and white clad girls alternately placed between the brown khaki clad boys, all quiet but bristling with pride, walked in single file and by classes to their allocated places in the large and now unfamiliar school room. And looking on were their teachers who all sported never before seen white blouses and shirts tucked into regulation black skirts or trousers, according to gender. Then following a swift registration and heart-felt prayers, fierce warning glances were thrown from the narrowed eyes of teachers towards well-known troublemakers, and the stage was set at last.

Now the children, their small hands lying submissively one on top of the other in their laps, waited and focussed their eyes on the spot in the corner of the stage from where they knew their visitor would emerge. And finally, after the headteacher's introduction which told them things they already knew – where the visitor was from, where he'd been, his kindness in coming to visit them, and blah blah blah – he stepped aside, the curtains in the far corner moved, and the long-awaited visitor was here at last!

First they saw the tip of one shiny shoe and then his whole body appeared. Then their palms, which had waited impatiently for this moment, unfurled and made rapid contact with each other, producing a deafening explosion of thunderous applause as the longed for one made his swift journey across the recently polished boards of the stage which rose just above their heads. On and on he came; and their eyes followed him and raked over him ravenously as he moved swiftly towards them. They noted his wide smile and sparkling eyes and without any awareness of doing so, their small bodies leaned forward in welcome, while their heads , also unknowingly, gently nodded as they studied him from head to foot and waited for his first words.

'Hello children' he said warmly. And so began their love affair of the man, and of his accent and of the word 'Hello'. And they in turn, shaped their own small mouths into unusual circles as if about to burst into song – just as he had done - and in a thunderous and lilting Jamaican accent which they hoped echoed that of his English one, they roared the totally new word of greeting as best they could with their own 'Hey-lo, Sir!'

He smiled, and they knew that they had done very well. And during his introductory speech about being a vicar in England he reminded them that they were all British citizens and were all governed by Queen Elizabeth. And some with short attention spans, noted during his introduction, the sharp side parting in his well-oiled hair, his bright white shirt embellished with very thin black vertical stripes and the metallic strips which adorned the tip of his shiny shoes. To those children, this was all grist for the mill of later conversations, and for the drawings they would inevitably be asked to do long after the visitor had left.

Meanwhile, the listeners learned that his church was in a place called Brixton – a piece of news which produced amongst the audience some audible gasp. Because many had not only heard the name in conversations but had seen it written on the blue tripartite letters with the multi-coloured chevron stripes which regularly winged their way from parents residing in England. They had also spied it on the 'Return to Sender' labels on parcels that came stuffed full of promises and dreams just waiting to be realised. Parcels bearing more letters of love, English clothes, toys, brightly coloured tins of toffees, and best of all – English biscuits contained in large round flower-decorated tins. Biscuits full of textures, that not only tasted new and delicious but were sometimes wrapped in packaging that were as exciting as the wares they enveloped. Brightly coloured silky wrappings which once empty of their bounty, were licked clean and secreted away with other precious treasures to be revisited and admired until another batch arrived.

And in amongst the remembering, the entranced children

looked intently at the long-awaited speaker and wondered if he had maybe seen or indeed knew their parents, or their older siblings. And without any awareness, some sighed deeply and longingly for parents they only really knew from photographs of forever smiling people which hung on their living room walls. Then in their semi-reverie they heard him say 'Yes, and I was once a pupil in this very school!'. And following the short intake of breath, chins dropped disbelievingly onto chests, and from under hooded lids, glances with neighbours were exchanged, while others, forgetting the rule of sit-up straight, had visibly slumped forward as if suddenly winded by an invisible hand.

'Yes,' their visitor continued 'I was a schoolboy friend of your headmaster.'

The information struck deep, and once more the eyes of his audience roved over his face, over his sleek black suit, the well-made jacket and matching trousers with its high waist and three outward pointing pleats all held flat by a black and brown plaited belt. 'Yes' he said glancing quickly over his shoulder 'Your headteacher was my best friend here'. 'Yes,' he said as if sensing their disbelief, 'at this very school!'

And now eyes full of wonder watched them both, and marvelled as the two men nodded in unison and smiled at each other as he spoke of the games they used to play, the places they visited, and of the ambitious plans they had often shared; in spite he said, of his own difficult domestic circumstances.

And as the children drew their imaginary pictures, they heard him say 'When I was a boy here, I often had to come to school without shoes. 'Because', he continued 'my father sometimes had to choose between feeding his family or buying them clothes'.

And being children, they looked straight at his beautiful shoes and studied the embellishments already seen by some, noted the shiny leather and the smooth laces tied in neat bows which peeped from under his trouser cuffs; and they shifted in their seats with satisfaction. And they were all happy for him.

And while he spoke in his mesmeric tones, their little heads rocked back on small necks as they listened to his story of poverty and hard work which he said was bequeathed on a people left abandoned after slavery by their so-called masters, whose only parting gift he said was that of being given British citizenship. A gift he said that he as a young man with thousands of others had been forced to accept when there were no other choices. And like him, many had utilised that gift and emigrated to England for a better life. To help what many called 'The Mother Country' he stated, with an undefined emotion in his voice.

As he spoke he might have noticed that on the faces of the boys standing at the very back, there was an eagerness of expression which suggested that his words had awoken in them the beginning of a dream – one not dissimilar to the ones that had wafted through or gripped the minds of the generation that had left to search for a better life. And many boys stood there and indeed contemplated that they too could travel to a place called Brixton or even to places they had heard of through snatches of conversations. America – The Bronx! Or Cuba maybe. They too, they thought, could be just like the man who stood before them so confident, so debonair, with his nice clothes, his expensive shiny shoes and his mouth full of fancy words in a fancy accent. Yes, maybet they too could broaden their horizons to distant shores and earn more than a daily living from the land to which their parents, and even their grandparents had been teethered.

And amongst the big boys known to the system as the failures of the yearly exams, this dream, newly implanted, was detected by an almost indiscernible shifting of the shoulders, a rising and tilting-back of the head and a thrusting forward of the chest by the smallest degree. And it was as though while staring into the face of the man standing in front of them, they imagined wearing his suit – just in a smaller size.

And as was the nature of these events, there were often unexpected results. Because the girls, many destined through lack of opportunities and finances to becoming young mothers or helpers around the homes of others more fortunate than themselves, now silently pondered on their blameless school records and their skills in essay writing and recitations which always elicited rousing applause from their audience. And so they too looked ahead and mused 'Why not me? Why not me indeed! I too could broaden my horizons'. And by simply conjuring up a dream of success on that day, many achieved it in later years.

And the speaker, now pausing for a moment, studied the upturned faces of his audience. The beautiful faces of the children that ranged in colours from polished black to sun-kissed white, and he gauged their receptivity, and saw that it was good, because they too looked back at him, smiling. Waiting for his next revelation.

'So', he began 'I have been back here for some months and I have made some valuable observations.' Then sounding almost like a benevolent uncle at someone's birthday party, he said he had come to give them a present, in the form of some valuable advice. And intrigued as only the very young whose sensibilities are rooted in fairy stories can be, they, especially the seven, eight and nine years olds watched him with heightened expectations and shifted optimistically in their seats. Maybe, they mused, he was about to tell us how to get some free sweets; and they glanced eagerly and with wide knowing eyes and broad smiles at their neighbours while with bated breath they prepared themselves for the magician's big reveal. For the rabbit hidden in the hat. For the abracadabra moment.

But unexpectedly he said, 'Put your hands up, and let me see who doesn't attend school when it rains?'

His audience smirked knowingly as if the instruction was a prerequisite to the game. And so as one, they grinned and flung their hands into the air with pride. And some of the younger ones with age-related missing teeth, grinned even wider; and swollen with pride in their burgeoning knowledge, they wiggled their airborne fingers enthusiastically, hoping they would be specially applauded by the black Englishman for their brilliance. But his sudden instruction to 'Put down your hands. All of you!' startled them. And they shifted uneasily in their seats and looked at him anew, wondering what they had done to displease this new hero.

Now speaking slowly and precisely and nodding as if he had caught them out in a quiz, he said 'Yes. I have noticed that you children here in Jamaica like to stay in your bed when it is raining!' Then after a short pause he chuckled slyly before adding in a conspiratorial tone "Yes I know! I know rain sweet yu!"

On hearing the Jamaican word at the end of his last sentence, they looked keenly at him and wondered fleetingly if his utterance was a question, a statement or a joke. But being devoid of uncomplicated thoughts or deviousness, they decided to nod enthusiastically at the assertion. But too late! They had offered the wrong response and now to their horror, it received a triumphant 'I knew it!'

As they recoiled with regret, he continued 'Yes! I know only too well that rain sweet you all!'

And while the Head looked across the stage at him as if he was John the Baptist The Second, he wagged a rigid finger at them and spoke in what many had decided was a dangerous tone. 'Let me tell you something children' he said, 'for Jamaica to grow, you must all stop that nonsense of staying in your bed when you hear a drop of rain sprinkling on your rooftops'. And after a pause in which they could hear a pin drop – if one had been thrown – he asked in a more conciliatory tone 'Do you hear me children?'

Now they, seeped in the knowledge of rain and all that it entailed nodded and thought of the last downpour they had experienced. And they recalled, some with a smile playing over their lips, of how they had at first witnessed the rain's appearance. How they'd seen a quickly growing and frantically advancing misty white cloud on the horizon, and on the scream of the word 'Rain' by a frantic adult, all members of the family had run wildly – the children laughing and squealing all the while – grabbing receptacles large and small, pots, pans, buckets, and set them in the open air and under the slope of roofs to catch the deluge that was rushing at speed towards them. And then many had watched with glee as the first heavy drops almost as large as saucers had fallen and splashed onto their bodies with a ferocity that quickly soaked them through before their escape, and then battered hard at the windows from which they now looked out. Then all safely contained within, they had listened as the drops had thundered out their rhythms on the soil, and against the metal and dull sounding plastic of the receptacles. Then the silence. And then they knew even before looking, that each vessel was now full and overflowing.

And the rain also brought an instant writing surface created by their warm breaths on the window! One on which they could draw, write, erase, and repeat time and time again. Their sums. The ABC. Capitals and lower-case. The spelling of names and places. Lessons they had learnt. Words heard and enjoyed. Spellings for future tests. The playing of teacher and pupils. And even teacher's names. And the drawings of things they had seen or imagined. Oh, the joy of unleashing their imagination on that small but neverendingly-giving surface. What fun! How they loved the instant theatre. And the feeling of cosiness which the rain had brought.

Being country children, they had also enjoyed listening to the sounds created by the rain as it had beaten down on the different types of vegetation, especially the drumming it made on the large oil-cloth surfaces of the banana leaves. Boom, boom, boom went the sound and they had watched as the huge leaves rocked and danced and swayed under the force of the relentless downpour. And always, one of the onlookers would heighten the fun by mimicking the movements of the leaves with their own gyrations, sparking an immediate competition to produce the most outlandish permutations.

Now the dreamers heard the speaker reminding them of the benefits of the rain while coaxing them not to be seduced by it. But in an instant they were being seduced and were recalling the sweetness of the raindrops at night as it fell on their roof, sounding like a million tap-dancing birds above their heads, and so caused them to fall into a deep slumber until morning. But once again, the voice of the visitor broke in on their delightful reveries. And it was saying 'Yes, as a schoolboy I always noticed that this school was always half empty on rainy days. That is sometimes for the whole of October and sometimes parts of November'. And at the sound of his accusing voice they reluctantly dragged themselves from their warm beds to which they had retreated and stared at him with slightly glazed expressions. And after exasperatedly running one hand through a non-existent beard, he turned briefly to his old friend the headmaster – who also bore on his face a surprisingly relaxed expression – and asked him while also nodding his head in agreement with his own statement, 'Wasn't that so Mr.Wilson?'

And Mr. Wilson, after breaking into a misplaced half smile as if suddenly disturbed from his own reverie, nodded his enthusiastic response, and then more soberly agreed 'Yes, you're right, Mr Roy. Year after year.'

Following the brief exchange, he then looked sternly at his audience and while rapping his hands on the lectern in time with his words he said 'Children- you – must – stop – wasting – almost – two – good – months – of – your – education – each – year. And come to school in the rainy season!' he finished briskly.

At this pronouncement, his audience looked up at him as if seeing him for the first time. Some sat opened mouthed and gasping while others shifted in their seats with what seemed to be acute discomfort. And inside each of them was a burning need and a desperation to remind the visitor of the age-old rule. The one passed down without modification through the generations. The one he did not seem to know. So, they stared up at him and wondered if he really was a real Jamaican. Because they had decided, silently and collectively, that he simply could not be one if he did not know the disastrous outcomes of cold water accidentally falling onto a warm body - especially if it was left there to dry!

They had all at some point of their so far short lives, languished undetected in half-lit corners or in adjacent rooms, and listened to their elders tell terrifying tales of rain-induced coughs which had swiftly developed into raging fevers and then turned quickly into funerals. And they had listened to questions regarding the cause of death and heard in their terrified state, the answer delivered in a hoarse whisper 'Den me no tell yu say a rain kill im?' causing the invited audience to exclaim in disbelieving tones 'Lawd Gad have mercy!' And the silent listeners, chock full to the brim with horror, had involuntarily heard other equally distressing tales of people who had ironed like they'd never done before, and following this marathon had triumphantly rewarded themselves with a refreshing shower. After which said the tale-teller, they were no more.

So steeped in such tales of sudden deaths, the children now listened to the visitor while throwing surreptitious glances at their teachers who they hoped would intercede on their behalf and remind the visitor of the rules. But then as if he'd read their thoughts, he said in a soft ameliorative voice, 'Yes, I can see you are all worried. And yes, I am a Jamaican too and I know how rain is feared in this country'.

His audience sighed, and many suddenly sat up straight. He continued 'I know the fear the population have of sitting in wet clothes and waiting for it to dry. Many of his audience threw desperate eye-rolling glances at their peers. 'So no, children' he continued 'I'm not asking you to walk in the rain and sit in wet clothes all day. They sighed with relief and he was their hero again.

He knew that once more he had them in the palm of his hands and so he continued 'Believe it or not, I was once a child! And maybe on some rainy nights I too had prayed for rain to continue until the morning. And sometimes my prayer was granted. But quickly he countered 'But I never gave in to the temptation to stay in my bed! Not once! Why?' he asked, then answered, 'Because I wanted to be somebody. Like you, I was desperate for an education, deperate to better myself. And using the tone of voice which had earned him the souls of many from the confines of the pulpit, he said 'So children, let me tell you this. 'Rain on zinc will not get you a job'. He paused. 'Rain on zinc will not put food on your table when you grow up'. Another pause. 'And unfortunately,' he paused for the briefest of moments 'rain as sweet as it is on the zinc, will not get you an education if you stay in your bed.'

Then he asked his audience an unexpected question. 'Have any of you children ever seen inside a freezer?'

Now whether because of their past experience of giving the wrong response, or simply not having had the pleasure of looking inside that appliance, or just happy to hear that the subject of rain was dead, most hands were kept firmly in laps. But he continued anyway 'Well in England, that ice which you see in the freezer is, in its softer state called snow'. Eyes like saucers bore into him as he continued, 'And every winter this snow lies thick and treacherous, not in the freezer,' he paused, 'but on the ground!'

Now his audience visibly trembled and as one, breathed in deeply. Yes! they thought, this is what we've come for! The new words, the new information, being transported to new places! And with their small hands clasped one on top of the other in their laps again, they licked their lips and braced themselves. All ready and prepared to be taken on a magical mystery tour. Then in the mesmeric tones of a storyteller they heard him say, 'This snow, it lies in every yard, and on every street. Sometimes for days.' He paused. 'Sometimes for weeks.' He paused again. 'And sometimes... even for months! That is until the sun decides to show its face again and melt it all away.'

And the children, still caught in their globes of magic, took a second to drag their eyes away from him and cast a puzzled glance at their neighbour, to query what he meant about the reappearance of the sun. But since there could be no discussion, question or explanations, they placed the puzzle into a pocket of their memory from where it would later be extracted, examined and possibly answered by someone amongst them who knew everything.

'Yes!' he continued 'and despite this snow, children in England still go to school every day'. And an audible ripple of horror ran amongst his audience, and he capitalised on it. 'Yes!' he said, 'this thing, this snow, is so cold, that it makes your toes and fingers sting.' And he added some familiar imagery, 'Just like when yu cut yourself and pepper gets into it before it fully heals.' Now there was a noise like a sudden gust of wind 'Ssss!'

He continued, 'And after the stinging, your fingers go numb. And even though you might still be able to see them, you cannot feel them. Imagine that!' He added dramatically.

He waited for the devastating information to sink in, then said 'I probably shouldn't tell you this, but... he paused and watched as they panted and nodded for him to Yes, tell them, tell them! And so with a hint of resignation in his voice he continued 'Some people who get very cold, even lose their fingers.'

'Sssssss!' Resounded around the room again. And such was the expressions of horror on each face, that it could have been surmised by any onlooker, that even without his audience being the beneficiaries of a film directors' imaginings, the scenarios they conjured up far outstripped any Hammer Horror production. In fact, conversations held long after the event revealed that their interpretation of what was said consisted of lifeless bodies lying in freezers amongst the lollies and ice creams – minus their digits.

But there was more to reveal. 'And this snow', he continued 'which is freezing cold, also turns their breath to smoke'. And now full faced connections were made with their neighbours in whose eyes they saw their own horror reflected. And since the vicar now rubbed his palms together after saying the word 'freezing' they also without being aware of it, emulated his actions. And as if in sympathy, mirrored his raised shoulders, and what appeared to be his laboured breathing. And some even glanced down to view the imaginary smoke which they expected to see issuing from their open mouths.

'And worse than this!' the speaker broke in as if he himself was elsewhere experiencing the inclement conditions of which he spoke. 'After a while, this snow turns to blocks of ice'. At this revelation they visibly flinched. 'And this ice he said, has the power to make people slip and slide and even to sometimes fall over'. And they grimaced as they imagined the characters in their reading books battling against these debilitating and devastating conditions.

Now after silently surveying his audience keenly, the speaker continued 'So children, next time it rains here, just think of the babies and the children in England struggling in the snow'. And his audience, some now close to issuing sympathetic tears, nodded. 'Yes, he said, think of them. Their noses red and cold and their little fingers numb and brittle. Think of them slipping and sliding and putting themselves in mortal danger.' He paused. 'Just to get to school'.

And as they stared back at him, wide-eyed, he advised them 'So when the rainy season comes, get yourselves out of that warm cosy bed and go to school.' 'No, I'm not asking you to step out of your houses into a raging downpour and walk to school'. You and I know that the rain stops and starts. And we know that when it stops, the sun always comes out'. Now the children smiled and nodded enthusiastically with each other, validating his statement.

'So', he continued, 'what I want to suggest is that on those rainy mornings you can get up and get ready in your school clothes at your usual time and have your breakfast'. His audience listened expectantly. 'Then as soon as the sun breaks through the clouds, you can set out for school as fast as you can. And he opened his arms expansively. The children seemed to like this idea and once again they nodded enthusiastically. 'That way you won't be missing a whole day of your precious schooling!' He smiled triumphantly and glanced at the teachers as he added while nodding 'And believe me, your teachers will be very pleased to see you. How do I know this? Because no teacher likes to sit in an empty classroom all day'. Some of the teachers smiled in agreement with his summary.

'So go to school!' he said, 'Even if there is still a bit of water on the ground. Believe me, splashing in a little water now and again is not going to kill any of you lovely children. The worse it will do is to wet up your shoes. But you can always carry those until you get to school' he chuckled.

At those words, the children nodded their small heads even more vigorously and enthusiastic murmurs could be heard up and down the rows. And while they offered him proof that his words had convinced them to change a habit of a lifetime, still his voice rolled on. 'So now, before I leave you, I want you to make a pledge to yourselves...and to me, and to your teachers. Make a promise that you will try your very best to get to school on the next rainy day. So please repeat after me. And then he said the most amazing words they'd ever heard.

He said in a voice loud and clear 'Rain will not kill me'.

Tentatively and without conviction they repeated his words. But then after several takes they gave back a resounding delivery which was aided by the swinging of his baton-like forefingers

Rain will not kill me!
Rain will not kill me!
I will not allow rain to spoil my future! They sang out.

And the force, power and conviction of their chants rose up towards the lofty ceiling, and finding no escape there, floated out through the numerous open windows, travelled up and over the grassy slopes, leapt over the picket fence and into the passing ears of the people on the Content Road, causing one surprised passer-by to say to another 'Bwoy, me neva hear dat before! Say rain caan kill yu…'

And the other replied with a slight raising of his shoulder 'But a school a say it, so it mus be true. And both shook their heads in consternation before continuing on their way.

Following his rousing speech, the visitor after stating most convincingly that his audience would be great ambassadors for the future of Jamaica, and after receiving his present, wrapped up with warm and effusive thanks, he received what could have been the most thunderous applause of his life. And although seeming on the verge of what looked suspiciously like tears, he produced what to his audience was the broadest of smiles they'd ever seen. Then bidding them a heartfelt 'Goodbye', accompanied by a cheery wave, he turned on his immaculate heels and disappeared behind the curtains. Just like the magician they believed him to be.

***

Two months after the memorable event, and long before the hand-written posters bearing the rousing words of the pledge had been taken down, the children witnessed the tell-tale clouds in the distant hills. And it was during the torrential downpour that they had remembered their promise and so had prayed fervently for a rain-free day.

But at dawn the flooded conditions did not deter the small bands of children who walked purposefully and at speed through the wet vegetation and along the wet roads in their bid to honour their promise to the Rain man. And their breaking of the long-held rule was witnessed in every hamlet and their chants were heard by all who saw them pass. Loud and full of fervour, the words, new to everyone who listened with disbelieving ears said quite clearly over and over again

Rain will not kill me!
Rain will not kill me!
I will not allow rain to spoil my future!

And it was known amongst one group of chanting children that their friend Cassie who lived at Pleasant Farm, had on that overcast morning declined the offer of a lift from her grandfather and had instead insisted on walking to school with her friends. And it was also noted that with shoes in hands, they had happily splashed in the rivulets of water that swirled around their feet.

And all who watched and heard the chanting children said in wonderment 'In all my born days a neva see or hear anyting like dat. God bless dem'. And they too repeated the amazing words they'd overheard.

But unknown to them, it had been the visitor, given the nickname 'Rain Man from England' together with the unknown substance called snow, which had created the fervour, the rousing chant, and the dismantling of a long-held belief.

Duppies

Now before we go any further, let's get something straight. In Jamaica what are known as ghosts in most parts of the world are in the typical contrary style of Jamaicans, known by another name – Duppies. And Jamaican Duppies pride themselves on not only having a different name but also in being the fiercest and baddest variety in that often dark and shadowy world.

And for most Jamaicans it is not just the activities of these creatures, for want of a better term, which sets their teeth on edge but also the mere uttering of their very name. For most people just saying those two syllables – even through hardly moving lips – will create in them a feeling of anxiety, tremors, and paroxysms of fear. And if an onlooker were to carefully study the person uttering such a name, they might even detect an ashen pallor on the surface of a previously healthy visage.

So yes, Jamaican Duppies feel themselves to be different from the usual vampires, slavering dogs or misty white sheeted haunting variety of spectres that display themselves on lonesome moors, in abandoned buildings or occasionally in the bedroom of a stately home where they had met their grisly end. And unlike other such entities, they're not content to be figures of fun talked about and disparaged as fixtures of an imagination addled by drink. Their aim is to be seen solely as malevolent creatures who can be viewed individually, in all their horrible configurations, by as many people as possible, and at any venue they choose. The only thing it is thought that these spectres have in common with their fellow creatures in other parts of the world, is their penchant for roaming at night; a time they use to conduct their most bone chilling terrorising which is often thought to be the cause of numerous unexplained heart attacks, sudden discoloration of hair, or the creation of irreversible gibbering idiots created out of previously sane members of the population.

And where, we may wonder, does this fear of these creature emanate from? Quite possibly it is bound up with old religious beliefs and practices which travelled from Africa with our enslaved ancestors. And when combined with the evil practices and punishments of slavery, and the darkness of the countryside, the ideal conditions for the creation of vindictive duppies was created and forever entrenched in the memory of the populace.

So all over the island, and even amongst those who've emigrated to foreign lands, stories abound where a lone occupant of a house relaxing behind locked doors and windows, have suddenly found themselves in the company of an uninvited guest, with catastrophic results, including their sudden demise. And so drastic steps were taken to avoid the occurrence of unexpected visitations. Many citizens on the advice of astute middlemen who spotted a money-making opportunity, purchased what was seen by them as an insurance policy which came in the form of a flesh and blood alarm system - a big fierce slavering dog. And householders, having been convinced of the natural sixth sense of man's best friend to sniff out non-human presence, and then to seize and destroy it with blood curdling barks, snarls growls and vicious teeth, were happy with their large financial outlay as at last they were able to lead a less stressful existence, especially at nights.

However, despite these precautions being put in place, duppy stories – based on real facts – the storytellers insisted – have never ceased. Many, although containing the ingredients to create permanent insomnia, were nevertheless found to be highly entertaining to those of a robust constitution, if not thankfully, a finely tuned imagination. And the one thing all the stories had in common was a moralising component. Yes, it was through these frightening stories that certain individuals who had developed bad domestic habits like leaving their chores until late into the night, were forced into changing their negative behaviour patterns. And many duppy stories were told to drunkards during their periods of sobriety, or to men who were on the verge of ruining their families by their frequent late visits to betting establishments, or to men (again) who for whatever reason, consistently got home later than their families desired.

Many of these cautionary tales had as their main character, a malevolent variety of duppy called a Rolling Calf. And with such a name you would expect that one of the creatures main identifying characteristics would be its rolling gait. But quite confusingly, it does not. Its outstanding feature is that, probably because of its size, it sits. Sits at night, large and solidly either in front of a door about to be opened by someone about to embark on carrying out their delayed chores; or they wait around corners for someone who at that late hour should have been already ensconced in the bosom of their family. And with its vast inhuman size, and its blazing red eyes full of attendant sparks, there is the additional horror of it having the power of speech which all victims agree, is delivered in a menacingly deep and supercilious male voice. And in that tone it delivers a few well-chosen words to the effect of – but not as polite – 'What yu doing out here at dis time of night? – words which have the instant effect of either changing behaviour, hair colour, speech fluidity or mental faculties. And in many cases the encounter affects all four in one fell swoop.

But amongst all of these creatures is the highly feared duppy who disguises himself as a regular human being. Now he, after meeting the person at a gathering or along the way home in the dead of night, listens in silence to a story about a long-toothed duppy. At the punchline of the story which focusses on the length of the duppy's teeth, the duppy, masquerading as a human, interjects while displaying his own awfully long teeth and asks in a most nasal tone, 'What! Longar dan dese?' Of course, the real human, on recognising that his travelling companion through the darkness has been the said character from his story, suffers instant life-changing results which forever prevents him from engaging in his previous outdoor hobbies and interests.

But if there is no sympathy for the rogues within this story, then let us please extend a sympathetic thought to the children who take great delight in sitting in shadowy corners on verandas listening to these tales of horror. Because when the hour arrives for retiring to bed, they most of all, find that the imagery constructed by them during the story sessions, now returns to torment them before sleep eventually and thankfully claims them.

And it is known that the memory of those stories and their awful images often last a lifetime...

Boo!

The Top Ten

The end of the number one song coincided with the disappearance of the sun. And then night, without warning, unfurled, and like a black blanket, was thrown over the land. Suddenly all colour was obliterated, and familiar objects took on, under the cover of darkness, mysterious and frightening shapes with new connotations and interpretations.

And in that instant that day became night, the small child sent an on errand some time before the sun had set, became alarmed at finding herself away from home at this dark hour. And in a land where ideas about the supernatural resonated deeply with the populace, she now experienced a lurching sensation in the pit of her small stomach when she contemplated the journey that she alone would have to undertake. But the fear with which she had suddenly been afflicted and which made her small knees weak at every step, was not just what apparition she would encounter on her journey home but was also due to the knowledge that having failed to return home quickly as instructed, she would no doubt incur the wrath of her grandmother.

Too late, she now belatedly recalled the voice of the said lady issuing her stern exhortations. And in the silence of the darkness, it echoed above the sound of her beating heart: 'Cassandra your grandfather not well. Get dressed and go to the shap for me.' And as she had sprinted across the lawn, the age-old reminder of 'and don't let mi spit dry before yu come back' had been trotted out and served for her to be mindful of time. Now she remembered her breathless arrival at the shop in the clearing, and the feeling of joy as she had spied the group of children standing a little way from the laughing groups of adults. They were, like her, happy to be away from home and the jurisdiction of institutions and their incessant demands and rules. She had joined them, and they had all, as if in their own little world, talked as though each subject broached and dissected was of the utmost importance and had never been invented, or discussed before. And under the warmth of the evening, conversations were conducted with acute fervency and simultaneously produced copious amounts of raucous laughter which flowed unencumbered with not a thought of their evening chores like herding the livestock, fetching water from distant pipes, or in the case of Cassie, feeding the chickens.

So it was there in the clearing which was banked on each side by rising columns of trees that the people had stood, revelling in the benefits of being a closely knit community while the glow of the golden rays of the sun rained down and liberally coated their faces and the leaves of the surrounding trees with something akin to powdered gold. And the surplus of this downpour was so abundant, it even fell onto the tops of the red pantile roofs of houses and shimmered like golden flakes, highlighting their positions amongst the thickly set trees, as it set each one alight with a type of glowing yellow fire.

And it was also from that clearing that the people had heard a not unfamiliar sound. Its bell-like timbre had halted their laughter in mid-guffaw as again and again, it blasted its sound through the trees, and triggered their sleeping memory before filling them with delight.

'But weight!' one of the adults drawled, while sticking up an enquiring fore-finger in the air, almost as if they were testing the direction of the breeze 'Mi hear something.' And adults and children alike narrowed their eyes in heightened expectation as they too looked searchingly in the direction of the of the approaching sound

'Yu right!' a member of the adult group said in an awe-struck voice as a look of wonder spread across her face. 'Yes, A hear it to.'

'Yu hear it to? The first person asked, desperate to be convinced as an expectant smile spread slowly across her face also.

'Is dat time already?' another member of the group enquired. 'Time fly man.'

'A know!' retorted someone else. 'It seems like is only de adda day he come here' added the speaker.

And after throwing an askance glance or two at the speaker the crowd continued to peer with intensity towards the source of the distant jangling, as the thing not yet seen, wended its way swiftly towards them. Then someone seeing a tell-tale flash of white through the banks of trees, exclaimed in a jubilant voice 'Yes, dere it is!' And judging by the effect of those words on the crowd, a stranger would have surmised that what has been seen - whether animal, vehicle, or an early pre-Christmas Jankunno parade, definitely held some special significance for the welcoming party. But they would not have known why, whatever it was, was anticipated with such glee.

Now the atmosphere is electric and people, with hands shading their eyes, and necks craned at painful angles, peer with contorted faces into the distance, and move their heads from side to side in a bid not to lose sight of what they now know is a fast moving van hurtling at speed through the dense foliage towards them.

'Yes, a can see it!' says a jubilant voice.

'Yes! See it dey! See it dey!' says another

But not everyone can.

'Lawd me caan si it' someone complains loudly

A burst of laughter rings out at this admission and so all with rigid fingers assist in pinpointing the movements of the vehicle. Then suddenly there is a cry of desperation from one of the trackers 'Lawd me caan wait for it to come. It taking too lang.' And the speaker issues like a full stop to their desperation, a loud kissing of the teeth which has the fizz of a cold fish plonked in boiling oil.

'Me know me dear' someone agrees and continues 'Me live fa dis ting,' and while there is a ripple of laughter from the crowd, they never for a second take their gaze away from the moving shape, which all can now see is the Andrew Liver Salts Van.

The various groups of children grip each other's hands and waists as they continue to stare in the direction of the oncoming sound.

'You hear dat' whispers one member of the group.

'Yes, a hear it to!' Said the other, boldly and daringly using snippets of the adults-only dialect while relishing the disobedience of breaking the rules of grammar laid down by parents and school.

Then another emboldened by the response of the previous friend, extended the conversation and the daringness of rule-breaking by saying 'Yes, is lang time since A hear it'. And they all laughed slyly, while glancing over their shoulders at the distracted adults.

On and on it came at speed, and some, while they waited, referred back to its last appearance and to the driver of this magical steed

Someone ask 'Wha de name a de likkle driver?'

'No Leroy?' someone offers

'No, is Mr Sonny boy. Wha im call again?'

'No Boyish?'

'Dats right' said the speaker 'is Boyish'

And there are smiles all around with the recollection

'Im is boyish fe true to!' someone laughs. 'Im is nice and polite anytime im come here.'

'Yes, nice boy, man' someone adds in soft affectionate tones.

Then the bells are upon them and Boyish is smiling back at them through the large glass screen. Then following the greetings, the good-fe-si-yous and the how-de-dos, he reaches back into the vehicle before escaping for refreshments. And in an instant, the number ten of the hit parade floods out around them. It is what they've waited and thirsted after, and its loud and pulsating beat causes the crowd to erupt in a frenzy of movement that matches the level of their anticipation.

The onlookers note the transformative power of the music on some usually staid members of the community. One of these is a person who is known by all as a veteran complainer of aches and pains. Now, under the spell of the music they are transformed as they engage in creating the most fantastically intricate footwork which even rivals many of the younger dancers.

And there were many others not usually seen as the life and soul of the party – namely those with a permanent disaffection for anything that included the word fun or humour, and who on an almost daily basis gave constant negative commentary about a host of topics like: Prices, services, other shoppers, dogs, small children, and sometimes unsavoury comments about members of their own families. But now, under the spell of the music they could be seen not only wreathed in smiles but were now almost unrecognisable as they moved with gay abandon coupled with a frenzy usually only witnessed amongst youngsters determined to display their carefree natures.

Spotted close by and in a category of his own, was none other than the schoolboy Norbert Ellis; he who sometimes unwittingly garnered more than a reprimand for getting his sums wrong. Now in time to the music he exhibited permutations and musical calculations which indicated that his talents did not lie in his classroom computations. And alongside him was the widow Mrs. Brown who came to church every Sunday religiously clutching her large bible to her chest which was always well shaded by one or other of her wide-brimmed hats. Now without hat or bible, she displayed moves which disproved any previous suspicion that she had no knowledge of dancing. And with her eyes firmly closed and head thrown right back as though singing a favourite hymn, she produced loud finger clickings as she moved her ample hips. Also spotted in the throbbing crowd was Mr. Beckman who was known to walk with a limp but now seemed miraculously healed as he threw shapes on the dancefloor as though born again, and with no discernible disability as he matched every move to those of his dance partner's wild gyrations.

And as was the universal practice, the adults at various junctures also gave a portions of their attention and light-hearted approval to the dancing children.

'Gwaan pickney!' they said

'Gwaan!' someone else repeated

'Yes!' someone shouted with joy.

'Step it!' another commanded

'Yes, yes yes!' Someone jubilated with pride, before there was a final burst of laughter and they returned to exhibiting their own wild dancing styles to the last minutes of the penultimate song.

And at about the same time that comments of approvals were being distributed, and just before the beginnings of the number one song, Mrs O Walker back at Pleasant Farm, felt the beginning of a niggling worry as the sun had begun to hover on the distant horizon.

Then it was upon them. The song for which they'd all thirsted. The song which because of its countrywide popularity had held a stranglehold on the charts for what had seemed forever. Now it exploded around them with its familiar chugging sound and its familiar words. And with their legs planted firmly on the ground and their arms and upper body swaying to the beat, they threw back their heads and sang the words they knew as well as any familiar prayer

'Oh Carolina' they sang in unison

And the children added their voices with 'Bap! Bap! Bap!'

And once again the words, whether of a person or a country, rang out

Oh Carolina, followed by its repetitive bap bap bap.

And the song, through its relentless and jaunty beat, caused some to move their legs as though leisurely cycling while their hands swung back and forth in tandem. And others sought to perfect steps which had been practiced time and time again in preparation for moments such as this. Movements which saw them moving backwards and forwards to the pounding music while intermittently making little jumps as if gingerly avoiding something lying on the ground. And there were those who stood as if rooted to the spot while simultaneously moving their upper and lower bodies in two completely different directions while furiously clicking their fingers; and in so doing they attracted a small admiring audience.

And all being familiar with the construction of the song, they knew that the end was nigh. So every morsel of it was enjoyed to its fullest and in one voice they sang and performed to perfection, the prowl, the prance and the dance suggested by the lyrics, embellishing each sliver of the music with their own unique permutations and flavours.

And then it was all over.

And the crowd, adopting the pose of spent long distance runners, watched as Boysie emerged from the shop. A flurry of handshakes followed, together with copious expressions of thanks and well wishes, as well as the pressing of small gifts into his reluctant but still grateful hands, before he bid them a 'Laters' and disappeared all engines blazing into the pitch blackness of the Jamaican night. And soon after, the small child followed in his wake and finally found herself breathless and terrified, on the boundary of her home.

Now walking on the familiar turf along the gravel drive and with her face averted away from the dark cemetery with its headstones glistening in the faint rays of the rising moon and in the intermittent flashing of millions of peenie-wallies, she looked through the blackness of the banana walk and spied the glow of light from the veranda up ahead. She mused on the delicacy that she knew had been reserved for her in the adjoining room. But a sudden movement from amongst the trees instantly tethered her with terror to the spot.

But relief and joy spread over her when she saw, not the expected monster, but her grandmother. So naturally relieved, she acted on instinct and prepared herself to move swiftly towards her friend and protector. And it was as the toes of one eager foot pressed into the grass verge in its preparation to propel her across the chasm of the small gully which separated her from that very sought-after embrace, that she had heard the question 'Where the medicine a sen yu for dear?'

And it was in the very instant that she was about to take flight, that her sharp animal-like instinct, fine-tuned for danger, had detected in the words a missing note, an unfamiliar timbre within the voice. One she had detected at some other place and at some other time when she had fallen out of favour and had been chastised. And so in less time than it took to perform the blink an eye, she had deftly and without missing a beat, reversed her balletic pose, cautioned her eagerness for immediate comfort, and rocked back into an immobile state. And in addition to the sharpness of her ears she had instinctively and simultaneously ran a visual check, and had detected from a quick glance, a spark, a glint of danger and an unusual determination in the eyes of her grandmother. And yes of course – there had been the absence of that welcoming smile.

And the lady herself had through her own sixth sense, ascertained that the child had been unnerved and therefore that she too must make hasty reparations in a bid to achieve her aim. So gently stretching out a hand across the grassy divide of the drainage ditch, she said in her gentlest voice 'Come dear. Give me your grandfather's medicine'. But the child, still trusting her well-honed instinct of danger, moved further away while extending her arm in a bid to obey her grandmother's request. And in the process she proved her instincts to be correct.

Because now the lady, eyes glittering with unadorned anger and impatience, took what was an over-eager balletic leap over the watery divide in a bid to secure not just the item but also the outstretched hand of the now terrified child. And it was halfway through the execution of that leap – which for a lady of her stature and generous dimensions was a thing of beauty, she involuntarily revealed to the suspicious child, an item previously prepared for her eventual chastisement. Yes, due entirely to her energetic exertions, a coiled-up implement of not too flimsy a structure, namely a belt from one of the said lady's garments, became dislodged from its hiding place – namely from between her heaving bosoms – and revealed itself for all to see. Like a suddenly lit flare burning bright, it now stood precariously balanced near the neck of the now thwarted lady, not only revealing her duplicity but as though expressing its sympathy for the now terrified child.

Now further convinced that she was in mortal danger, the frightened child took an urgently executed backward leap while uttering the culturally forbidden word for children 'No!' And then using what could have been described by a cricketing pundit as an underarm throw, she launched the long-awaited medicine into the long grass and at the feet of her advancing pursuer, before creating even more distance between herself and the immediate danger. But as she made her escape out of arm's reach, the words she and countless other naughty Jamaican children feared the most, rang out and travelled towards her. And they said 'And if it's before you go to sleep tonight yu going to get a beating for keeping yu sick grandfada waiting'.

And in that moment, as the penitent child ran into the darkness to make a circuitous route home, she vowed never, ever again, to wait for the Andrew's Liver Salts Van.

Abracadabra!

I had trolled my grandmother all morning. Kept her in my sight right from the end of breakfast as she had huffed and puffed and bustled over getting the house tidy for the arrival of Miss Vie the cleaning lady.

And it was while I had silently watched and then stealthily followed her from room to room, totally undetected, that I had formulated and decided on my plan of action to resolve the mystery. But while waiting for a change in her busy routine I was disturbed by an unexpected explosion behind me. A sound which reminded me of fresh fish being plonked into boiling hot oil. A long drawn out fizzing sound. Reeling round in alarm to ascertain the reason for this sound of discontent, I had found the lady whose movements I had dogged, standing alarmingly close and towering over me. Bearing a disagreeable expression on her face, she proceeded to inform me in the unfriendliest of tones that my stealthy behaviour had been noted and that she would dearly like to know why I was sneaking around the place and following her. Surprised and discomfited at having been observed by the one under observation, I searched around my eight-year-old brain for an answer to put her off the scent.

'I...I...I'm trying to help you grandma' I stuttered.

'Help mi?' she bellowed. 'Help me how?' And after the tiniest of pause in which she indicated that she was not convinced by my answer, she continued 'Help me by following me with your two empty hands and looking at me as if you neva si mi before?' And again, she kissed her teeth, but this time with only a short sharp fizz before she resorted to dishing out the usual advice.

'Chile' she said, 'if you want something to do, go and tidy up your room!' Then like a ship set on a course for distant shores she circumvented me and sailed ahead while throwing some words over her shoulders 'And put all af your dirty clothes in the wash basket for Miss Vie'. Then that fizzing sound again.

Now, from habit and not in a tracking kind of way, I followed close behind her so as to ensure that I did not miss out on hearing the rest of her instructions.

'In dat way' she continued 'you can help everybady.' And then in a slightly growling tone she added 'Instead af using your time following me fram room to room like you fraid a duppy'. Another fizz.

And before she started to hum her favourite hymn, 'Rock of Ages cleft for me....' she asked her usual unnecessary question 'Yu hear mi Cassandra?'

Well I must have done, as she knew that I was right behind her. 'Yes Granma' I answered promptly, in a deliberately simpering tone.

So thwarted for the moment in my quest to play detective, I slinked off in the other direction under the guise of carrying out her bidding, but in reality, to consider my new plan of action. The one needed to solve the riddle that had presented itself to me the previous day.

It was yesterday when on awaking from my nap in the open air, I had become aware that although my eyes were closed, I still had the ability to see the dark waving fronds of the tree under which I lay. There they were, boldly silhouetted against the sky. I opened my eyes to prove to myself what I had just seen through my closed lids. I saw them! So I closed my eyes once again, just to be certain of what I had experienced. Yes! I decided that I could really see with my eyes closed! And as you can imagine, I was astounded! And it was then that I came to the realisation that I was in receipt of an extraordinary gift.

Now being only eight years old and having such phenomenal powers, had to my ever active imagination, so many possibilities. I could, I mused, become an invaluable teacher's pet – known to some as teacher's spy. And even more valuable would be my ability to appear to be fast asleep while witnessing the secret antics of adults in whose company I sat. With that gift I could, after learning their secrets, hold them to ransom! But first I decided to ascertain whether my grandmother in particular also had this amazing gift. And that was why today, I had to dog her every move. I needed to gather vital information about her powers of also being able to see with her eyes closed.

Yes there had been numerous occasions when she had surprised me by revealing knowledge of my movements and actions when I had been under the impression that I had not been observed. There had even been one occasion when she had detected through a solid wall, me reading one of her letters from England. But that I decided needed a different type of experiment and so was a task for another day.

Now the information I needed to gather to disprove my suspicions could only be gained during her mid-morning nap – the same time unfortunately that I was usually, against my will, forced to take mine. But not today. Today I needed to monitor closely the moment at which she not only entered her bedroom but the moment at which she fell into a deep slumber. Only then could I put my plan into action.

Before long, while listening from the confines of my room, I detected her making some preparatory sounds – the closing of curtains, various high-pitched yawns, and then just what I'd been waiting for, the faint creaking of bed springs as she lowered herself onto her side of her huge bed. Then rising up from mine, I prepared myself for gaining firm proof that I was unique.

After what I surmised to be about five minutes, I peeked through a chink in the slightly open door and noted her sleeping state with satisfaction. Her closed eyes, the sound of her regularly spaced breathing, the rising and falling motion in her chest area, and the best indication that she was in a deep sleep – the falling apart of her lips as witnessed in all heavy sleepers. At last! I could put my carefully constructed plan into action.

With the top half of my body thrust further into the room, I kept an eye on my prey. Then slowly and noiselessly manoeuvring myself through the door, I employed long stealthy steps on unshod feet and on tiptoe, towards the bed. Finally, I was there! Beside and towering over my sleeping grandmother! But once there, the unexpected urge to kiss her sleeping face almost overpowered me and caused me to abandon my plan. That of ensuring that she remained asleep throughout the operation. So, adopting a steely resolve in a bid to achieve my objective, I prepared to carry out the experiment that I had devised for her. A feeling of imminent success flowed through me and I knew that I was on the brink of an amazing discovery. Yes, I was about to discover what I had always suspected - that I was different and gifted; and that I alone was imbued with the ability to see through closed eyelids! So, emboldened with that knowledge, I prepared my fingers.

Stretching my body to its full height while keeping my eyes focussed on the closed eyes of the subject who lay sleeping below my hands, I proceeded to raise my fingers upwards while bending them into the shape of a crab, as had been demonstrated in a magic trick in one of my Sunday comics. And just as the series of pictures had indicated, I began to flex my rigid fingers in a rapid open and closed style while silently but through moving lips, I repeated again and again the word 'Abracadabra' while still furiously flexing my fingers. Throughout all this frantic activity, my patient remained fast asleep - as was expected – and so finally proved to me after my final flicking, that I alone had the special gift of seeing through closed eyelids.

But my thoughts and actions were suddenly and violently interrupted, as from below my petrified fingers came a most almighty roar as my sleeping grandmother, her face contorted almost beyond recognition and less than a quarter of an inch from mine, yelled in a voice full of terror, and to my tuned ear, a good proportion of extreme annoyance 'What yu doing here chile? You frighten de life out of me!'

With my fingers still frozen in the shape of a crab – and now located in the region of her ears – I was, needless to say, speechless. So I turned and fled without hesitation to the safety of my room where with some sadness, I imbibed the realisation that she too had the special power of seeing through closed eyelids.

But in spite of that knowledge, I still for some reason harboured a sense of satisfaction…

Party Animals

The creaking hinges of the distant iron gates to Pleasant Farm being opened, signalled to the highly receptive ears of those close by and those far away that the hour had come.

The sound had, like a distant monotonous hum coated in metal, reverberated through the flora and through the soil in which they stood, swept between the vast banks of trees, and then surged and bounded over the hills before it dived headlong down the green dales of the cow pastures, and was finally swallowed up, submerged and silenced by the rushing fish-filled silver river.

And the workers dotted around the distant contours of the farm, engaging in their daily tasks also heard the signal of iron on iron, and so received the unspoken message that not only had Mr. S Walker, proprietor, arrived at the entrance of the L shaped drive in one of his long fishtail cars, but also that their working day and their own homeward journeys to nearby hamlets, was nigh.

And following the sounding of the signal, a keen observer would have noticed a movement in the undergrowth amongst the grass, the shrubs and closely growing tangled weeds. And then they would have seen emerging into the open, first a few then a continuous flow of animals of every description, traveling at speed and hurrying towards a familiar location. And regular observers would have learnt that it was a ritual enacted at the end of each working day, except at weekends when Mr. O Walker either did not leave the farm or worked instead to an erratic timetable.

But today, this menagerie rushed on, their faces all pointing homewards, while their bodies moved smoothly and decisively and in rhythm, gathering speed as they progressed through the undergrowth. Some, like the feathered domesticated creatures in a desperate bid to escape the tangle of the vegetation, seemed to occasionally rise up above the brush, wings flapping furiously before returning to earth and charging homeward as they employed a rocking gait and their trademark long ungainly strides.

And alongside and behind, others travelled homewards with great urgency: running, careering, leaping up up up towards the large and welcoming blue house which stood solidly in the vast space, wrapped around on all sides by land gently meandering off in every direction. And as the first wave arrived, a door opens and reveals as it does each day, the occupants who have also heard the signal and know that soon there will be a gathering. It is the small party of three, Mrs. O Walker and her grandchildren Casandra and Errol. They step out and walk leisurely down the steps of the broad veranda and onto the lawn where they wait with expectant expressions on their faces.

And as the animals of every description journey through the fertile and ever-growing terrain, they move with relentless speed. But if they had in a leisurely moment paused to observe their surroundings, they might have encountered and inspected an ever thickening stalk meandering snake-like on the ground and which would have in turn led them to the large yellowing pumpkin – one of many along this fecund vine – lying heavily and quietly like a large round sleeping child. Half hidden, it lies, sheltered protectively by huge umbrella-shaped leaves, shading it from the overhead sun. And whoever discovered it would have marvelled at the sight of it lying there camouflaged by its leafy canopy.

Or on another day, after hearing the sounding of the signal, and if they had not been in such a desperate hurry to reach their destination, they might have paused and gazed up at the overnight growth of the large collection of bean stalks all steadily rising up their wooden supports. Structures which, at the very moment that they rushed by, were being slowly weakened by their lush and heavily laden passengers, the beans and peas all now swelling and ripening in the evening sun, and all, to the trained eye, on the verge of bursting from their shiny green tight-fitting velvet jackets. But not today, as the noses of the travellers are pointed straight ahead intent only on deftly avoiding obstacles, which when encountered, causes their groupings to separate then merge and coalesce as they navigate the lush density of the familiar terrain.

And apart from droves of chickens there are dogs of every description, many of whom on a daily basis travel singularly in pursuit of their favourite pastime of mongoose-hunting, but always, on hearing the distant signal, never fail to swiftly and decisively journey back towards the appointed meeting place – their ears pinned back as though caught in a terrible storm. And as with people, there would always be one canine, being a less industrious individual, who might have spent the warm afternoon lying and dreaming under the green shiny leaves of the small but heavily laden orange trees, having imbibed their citrus scent which had rendered him captive and docile. But now in spite of that, had at the sound of the signal and the purr of the distant engine, shaken himself from his torpor and risen on unsteady legs, stretched his body in all directions before finally moving swiftly uphill to join the gathering throng.

All gathered now in a frenzy of anticipation on the green

swathe of land which bedecks the frontage of the solid house, their heads turn in the direction of the oncoming sound to watch as the sleek purring vehicle manoeuvres its length around the curved angle of the L-shaped drive. And then as it makes its usual stop on the brow of the hill, the waiting quivering crowd, first sitting then standing and repeating this action, prepares like a troupe of first-night actors, to present their daily and very well-rehearsed show for their owner and benefactor Mr S Walker, and family.

Then as if on the downward stroke of an invisible baton, the welcoming party in their assembled ranks begin to emit a high-pitched conglomeration of noises which to the humans was an orchestra of beautiful sounds from their livestock: the numerous dogs, scores of chickens, a large clutch of spotted guinea chicks, a frisky pair of escaped piglets, and even some curious birds from the tops of fruit-laden trees had strayed down to investigate the noise. Then the creatures as they did each day and at the same hour, sang their gratitude and welcome to the driver who in turn sat with a broad grin spreading all over his handsome face as he repeated over and over again 'Oh boy! Oh boy! Oh boy!'

And then it was time for the welcome-home dance to begin. Moving to the chords of a silent music, the dogs began to cavort wildly, while all the time emitting their throaty ruff- ruff- ruffing barks. And the chickens with their cluckings and squawkings added another layer of bass, which was further embellished by the noisy repetitive singing of the birds overhead. Then the dogs at the height of their excitement, not content to just dance in a group, took it upon themselves to deliver a variation on what became known as the stoop-bottomed dance. This entailed the almost impossible feat of them moving rapidly (or not, depending on age) forwards then backwards, their bottoms almost dragging on the ground, while they desperately tried, unsuccessfully, to control their unwieldy tails. A display which never failed to generate volumes of laughter from their human audience.

Then adding to the cacophony, the mud-splattered piglets who had no doubt escaped through a permanently loose board, now like small mischievous children, squealed and whizzed around in an uncontrollable headlong manner while occasionally practicing their underdeveloped grunts. And in among the melee there would be the unexpected mooing of the cows who, penned in their distant pastures, were eager to make known their gratitude to their benefactor. And the dancing and the applause might have continued as before were it not for the arrival of the usual latecomer.

All eyes turn to note his arrival while Mrs O. Walker exclaimed "Yes! Here comes Mr. Show-off!' And as usual, wearing his trademark green and jewelled feather jacket and his silver crown, he glides forward on his long elegant legs, and like a supermodel, sinuously gyrates his long silver neck while he struts languorously towards the car and the still boiling mass of animals.

And there is no doubt that his vigilance informs him that he is closely observed by all and so he rewards his audience by suddenly – like a cloak-wearing magician – unfurls his elongated iridescent tail feathers as though they were a beautifully embellished pack of playing cards. And now still standing on the fringes of the melee like a newly crowned king, he waits to be joined by his slower less showy mate, the peahen.

Then as the sun begins to slowly crawl towards the horizon,

the entertainers receive the reward for which they have been waiting – their evening buffet. And following their much-deserved feast, they wander slowly back into the undergrowth to settle into their night-time abode until dawn.

Chucka
Chucka
Chucka

For Cassie, the repetitive noise that suddenly invaded her room as she lay in bed, caused her to suddenly feel a fear she had experienced only once before when she had been threatened by the murderous robber while on her way to the shops.

With her eyes staring into the darkness, and her thumping heart threatening to leap from her chest, she wondered at the source of the unusual repetitive sounds which seemed to seep through the walls. She held her breath and listened. And yes! There it was again. And each sound came in quick succession of the other. Chucka chucka chucka.

Striving desperately to identify its source, her eight year old mind wondered if it was the sound of birds on the roof. Or if it could be the swishing of the curtains that surrounded the large deep bath out of which she'd witnessed her grandmother struggling to get out of and vowing never to enter again. And then desperately clutching at straws, she wondered if it could be the sound of running water from the new contraption called a shower.

Finally, she drew the only conclusion most Jamaicans arrived at when they happened to experience anything of an unusual nature – that the source of the noise was being created by a duppy. That creature who everyone knew roamed at night inside and out and who made their main purpose of existence that of frightening the populace; usually when they were alone and out of the reach of other human beings.

Now hardly breathing and with her head and body underneath the sheet, she wondered why her grandparents had not rushed in to rescue her. Wondered, as a new wave of terror swept over her, if the duppie had crept up on them unannounced and turned them into statues. But she had learned from a wide variety of storytellers that the powers of these terrorisers were limited. Once when playing the role expected of all small children – to be seen and not heard – she had listened with interest and had learned that there was an antidote to the presence of duppies and their dastardly deeds. And while this antidote was not one available to well brought up children, she consoled herself with the hope that if there was any danger, her grandparents, even though they were the most politest of people, would, if they or her were in grave danger, use the antidote by speaking very bad language in the prescribed gruff and dismissive voice to make the creature disappear.

But it was the next instalment of a prolonged burst of 'Chucka chucka chucka! Chucka chucka chucka! Chucka chucka chucka!' that had sent her imagination reeling off into the stratosphere and convinced her beyond any doubt, that she was not only about to come face to face with the creator of the mysterious noise, but was also about to be grabbed by its gnarly hands and devoured in one gulp by its double rows of jagged yellow teeth. And it was this prospect that had not only caused her plaits to rise up from her scalp, but saw her leave her bed in one desperate movement which took her swiftly from the confines of her dark room – followed no doubt by the creature who now ran with outstretched arms inches away from her fleeing form – and into the bedroom of her grandparents where she arrived breathless and without the required ceremony of knocking. And there, sitting quite calmly in the yellow glow of her room was her grandmother, and yards away, the covered and not yet snoring, sleeping form of her husband.

And the now bemused and terror-struck child noted at once that the repetitive noise had ceased. And also that there was no monster. But yet limpet-like, she clung to her grandmother and buried her face into the warmth and safety of her body while her eyes as round as saucers, flooded with tears of relief. She listened to the soft words of comfort which rained down on her, and slowly, with her arms still wrapped around the shoulders of her grandmother, she began to speak haltingly and directly onto and into the concerned face of the lady who in turn listened in bemused silence to the tale of the noise. The repetitive noise which had issued through the walls and indeed from this very room. And it was that as the child spoke, the lady, still adopting the pose held when so violently interrupted – one hand frozen in mid-air and with her left foot resting on her right knee – had proceeded with her previous activity.

And just as the child was about to replicate the sound and conclude her story, she had looked down with blazing and unbelieving eyes as her best person in the whole world, the person to whom she was clinging for comfort and dear life, had swiftly and in bouts of three, drawn a rasping implement across the soles of her feet and created the very sound of the duppy from which she had just escaped.

'Chukka chucka chucka' went the rasping implement.

And exhibiting a mixture of fleeting terror and substantial relief in equal measure, the child, her legs now unable to support her, collapsed fully into the arms of her grandmother, as she uttered the only words that she could muster, 'Oh Grandma'.

Then during the quiet laughter that they shared, Mrs. O Walker, while continuing her beauty routine, breezily told her

‘Your madda sent it to me from England in the last parcel’. And added as she continued her routine ‘A don’t know how I did without it all dese years’.

And she stifles a chuckle as the child quietly replicates the sound created by the movements of her hands. ‘Chucka chucka chucka’.

Likkle Wicked

Mi push over mi Granmadda todeh" the stocky boy had announced in a defensive voice. And he had swaggered to his seat amongst the open-mouthed seven-year olds who sat beautifully dappled by the sun as it liberally distributed its assertive rays through the leaves of the large and fecund breadfruit tree.

And they, his classmates had collectively drawn in a deep and alarmed breath, before in one simultaneous movement, silently turned and pasted their frightened eyes him while they considered his shocking statement. They had studied him in his entirety: from the top of his neatly combed and side-parted hair, down to his khaki-coloured school uniform, on past his brilliantly oiled knees, and down to his shoeless feet. Then following this forensic inspection, they had whispered through cupped hands directly into each other's ears while still throwing furtive glances over their shoulders towards the now silent boy. And the job was done. Yes, it had been silently agreed that his nickname had to fit his heinous deed.

So thereafter he was known, as if newly born, as 'Likkle Wicked'.

The first part of this name attested to his small but wiry stature and the second part was their opinion of his actions. It was a nickname which, like all other such names, spoke of the bearer's deeds. These monikers were testament to major events in the owner's lives and would almost certainly remain a fixture unless they left and decamped to another parish or left the country all together. But many were revealed voluntarily by their owners and thereafter worn with pride, especially if it attested to them having carried out heroic actions.

As was the case with another boy from the school, long since passed into adulthood, who for many years had gone by his proper name of Denzel. But because of his amazing and many times proven ability to catch or capture a ball from any direction, even once one coming towards him from behind, he had been bequeathed, some say anointed, with the name 'Captcha'. And 'Capture' would not do, it had to be spelt in the Jamaican style. Anyone adopting what was called the speakey-spokey pronunciation would be laughed at heartily by all – including the owner of the name – who when outnumbered by the laughing crowd, would laugh at himself before adopting once more, the correct pronunciation. And as regards Captcha, even in old age he was known to answer to his moniker with pride and would gladly relate (but no longer able to demonstrate) to newcomers, including grand and great grandchildren, how he had come by that illustrious name.

So likewise, Likkle Wicked was destined to be forever known by that name which unfortunately attested to his unacceptable deed. And maybe because it was felt he deserved such a name, even teachers sometimes, once the demands of any legal document had been satisfied, requested his presence at their desk with the use of that name; the pronunciation of which caused them unintentionally to use during the working hours, a slight snippet of the language which was usually reserved for social events when among family, friends and other select familiars.

As time passed, even those who had known him prior to his new baptism could no longer remember his real name. The new name, which many had to admit had a ring of derring-do about it, had stuck like glue and had followed him out of the school gates each time he had ceremoniously or unceremoniously left. And because of its unusual combination of words and spellings, it led to him being known well beyond the confines of his domicile and later even to the outreaches of Tower Isles, Ocho Rios and beyond to the Hills of Stoney and Breadnut and Fern Gully. And even further when some of his friends and acquaintances travelled to England…

And among the relatives of the children who had heard the story of how he was bequeathed the name, he was designated to being of 'bad breed' who would come to nothing. Then on finding no answers to questions regarding which church he attended, his actions were deemed as belonging to the wickedest of abusers, and so along with wild shaking of heads, tuttings and outright kissing of teeth, dire predictions of a hopeless future were made. But all added that they would remember to pray for his likkle soul, even though he had been marked down by all the morally upright predictors as beyond redemption. And in addition, the children of these people who were well versed in premonitions of doom were warned with more wagging of fingers, and askance glances when the culprit was close by, to keep away from him in case he tainted them and dragged them into bad company and deeds – which were of course, always the faults of others.

Time passed, and the boy formerly known as Cedric, changed. Maybe it was because of those prayers being sent up daily on his behalf, or some said maybe because of the gradual emergence of his natural charm – which was usually disarmingly accompanied by a rascal's grin by which he displayed a fine set of strong teeth. Now older, taller, and more muscular, the name Likkle Wicked became rather a misnomer, as he became renowned for his kind nature. Whether his new behaviour was designed to seek atonement or was just as was previously said , the curative powers of time or prayers, every action he performed – unless he was wronged or assaulted – overflowed with kindness to those who were weaker, smaller or just younger than him. He also became in many disputes, a skilled negotiator, conciliator, and moderator who was praised on many occasions for calming heated discussions which seemed to be teetering dangerously on the brink of physical entanglements. And eager to see new-found friends on Sundays he also became a regular churchgoer and was hailed as a reformed character by the vicar, former naysayers, and also by a delighted murmuring congregation who nodded, raised their grateful eyes to heaven while fanning themselves and mouthing the words 'Thanks to God' each time he crossed their paths.

But his fame as a hero were not just in matters of disputes or among the church congregation. No, he also became known at school as a benevolent breaker of almonds for the younger children. Yes, many a morning break would find him installed at the front of a queue, his head with his trademark light brown hair, bent over a large rock around which knots of small girl and one or two small boys stood, each holding tightly in their palms, an unbroken almond. Their friend Likkle Wicked they knew would release the contents, not all crushed as when done by some others, but with the nut intact and ready to be consumed without the inconvenience of having one's tongue being ripped to shreds by bits of shell. Yes, he was the one to whom each would utter in the most simpering of tones after the nut had been released back to them 'Tanks Likkle Wicked'. And he in turn would take a moment to flash his film star smile upon them before he returned to vigorously cracking and releasing the next nut for his fans.

But time as they say waits for no man – or boy.

The years flew by and soon it was time for everyone, including some despairing teachers, to say goodbye to Likkle Wicked. So, with great fanfare and some actual tears he, along with his come-of-age peers, was sent off with kind words and some mementoes, into the big wide world.

The new term began with the children standing in their usual assembled spot while the headteacher, Mr. Wilson stood like a regal lion in his usual place on the top step and facing the distant street where the families of his pupils carried on their daily lives. Behind him stood his retinue of stern-looking staff who as usual stood ready to narrow their eyes at anyone brave or foolish enough to move a muscle. But today, instead of their incessant roving, or focussing somewhat challengingly on the new siblings of known troublemakers, they seemed instead to be fixated on something or someone at the very back. And those pupils brave and bold enough to take a quick backward glance, after accurately following the direction of the teacher's gaze, noted to their delight that the figure was none other than their friend and mentor, the one and only... Likkle Wicked!

A whisper here and there and then a frisson of excitement ran like electricity amongst them. Yes, there he was! Dressed in the regulation khaki uniform and looking slightly taller, he stood in the space where boys like him who had failed an important exam usually returned and planted themselves – in the very back row. And now with his face looking like an angel and what some with a broader vocabulary would have said was a smirk, playing on his lips, he stared innocently ahead of him.

Now coincidentally, it was the week that Likkle Wicked re-joined the school, that the American fizzy drinks company entered the lives of the community in a bigger than usual way. So, to relay to you dear reader how such an event impacted on the island, we will leave the returning Likkle Wicked striving to gather the knowledge which would eventually avail him of that illusive certificate, and instead, narrate to you, the machinations of this competition and its effect on the people.

This dark coloured drink, tailor-made for sun-drenched locations, and usually depicted on billboards in tall glasses full of ice, with a profuse collection of bubbles trying desperately to escape from its surface, was regularly and in vast quantities on account of the weather, copiously consumed by the populace. And many of those consumers would often imagine themselves to be Americans lounging luxuriously on golden sands whenever they imbibed its exotic flavour. And children too just loved it for its taste which complimented perfectly the popular and delicious yellow cake, bun, or Bulla cake to which they were all extremely partial. But now this drink was to have a bigger than usual impact on everyone's lives as they were now being promised the possibility of gaining rewards with every bottle bought – even if not consumed.

Prior to the competition, the bottle top would be hastily discarded in a bid to access the cold bubbling liquid, but now during the time of competition, each purchaser of this amazing drink, prized the lid as if that itself was now made of pure gold. So now, the bottle after being opened, would be put aside with the brown beverage untouched. And the purchaser, sparks of hopes already issuing from their eyes, would enthusiastically set to prising out the cork from inside the confines of the lid where lay the source of all their dreams in the form of a letter of the alphabet. The missing one that would now complete the uncompleted word already in their possession, and thus gain them that until now, elusive item promoted by the drinks company.

So, because of this desperation for items that prior to this time they had not known even existed, the old tried and tested national quencher of any raging thirst – water became unfashionable, and overnight became the preserve of very desperate second-class citizens. And to that end, the liquid's superior qualities were flaunted by a forest of hastily constructed larger than life hoardings, which were not only placed in the usual high street positions but also in surprisingly obscure rural backwaters and previously unknown locations. And all depicted images of hands busily engaged in distributing huge gushing quantities of the brown liquid flowing over cubes of ice while the desperate eyes of the soon to be recipients gawped at the wasted bubbles.

And regarding the prizes! On many billboards up and down the land, were pictures portrayed in a horn-of-plenty style, of priceless gifts tumbling forth. These included indispensable items such as pen sets, gleaming pots and pans, pillow sets with matching quilts – an item which was surprisingly craved my many housewives, and domino-sets, which because of its two syllabled name, seemed to need a whole load of letters. And the benefits of all these prizes were extolled in ringing phrases by the company as destined to bring unimaginable happiness to their lucky recipients. Kitchen items were depicted as being so labour-saving that not an ounce of energy had to be expended in the creation of delicious and unrecognisable delicacies, and items promising new leisure activities not normally engaged in under the heat of the Jamaican sun – golf being one of many –

indicated through its set of small balls and dangerous looking clubs, that life could be a breeze all year round, after the winner had of course invested in some strange looking shorts and scratchy looking vest and cap.

But there was one prize for which many young and not so young participants, dreamed and thirsted after. And many would gather regularly and spell out the feats that they would accomplish if they had this revered prize in their possession. Of how the hours in a day would increase if they were to gain this item and how their horizons would stretch way beyond the boundaries of their locality. The surprise they would give to long lost relatives with their sudden appearance, and the new distant job opportunities that would be opened to them with this new possession. Oh, and the vast wealth they would accrue on acquiring it. The big entrepreneurs they would become. And of the weddings, cars, and children they could then afford if only they could acquire this fantastic item. Oh, if only they could win the main prize. The shiny steed. The bicycle!

However, there was one major impediment preventing them from achieving their dreams of owning that much sought-after vehicle. And that was the scarcity of the letter Y which would fill the gap in their spelling of that magical seven-letter word. So at the instantly recognisable fizzing sound of a bottle of the refreshing drink being opened, a hush would fall upon the room and all eyes would immediately be turned onto the purchaser who was on the brink of being lucky. Breaths would be tightly harnessed, and hearts would pound harder, as the inside cork adorning the bottle top was hastily peeled away and discarded to who knows where. And with their eyes fully focussed on the searching eyes of the potential winner, they waited for the cry of jubilation, for the tearing up and down and around the shop, for the endless grin of someone who had discovered the magic letter.

But no. Once again, there would emerge only the familiar cry of despair and sometimes palpable rage from the tortured depths of the sagging frame. And many purchasers after discarding their unwanted letter would, often in less than gentle voices, express the view that 'dat blasted saaf drink company nat making any Y and a nat gwine badda wid dem anymore'. And having made this vow of forgetting about them and their product, many would indeed cease buying the bubbly liquid…that is until they remembered their redundant stash of six letters for which they had paid a king's ransom. And so, after a short respite, the practice of collecting would again begin in earnest. Sometimes with more urgency, more desperation, and indeed a larger outlay of funds than before.

But some, still harbouring intangible feelings of hope, took to disseminating reports of where many Y's had been found or were likely to be found, and some would even make a special pilgrimage to named towns – only to be seen returning at a late hour – disconsolate, disheartened and badly in need of a cool bubble-filled drink. And sometimes there were newspaper reports alongside grainy pictures of people who had found the elusive letter and could be seen dressed to the nines and leaning nonchalantly on their prized bicycle. But try as they might this lucky winner could never be traced in any part of the island to confirm their win.

And so those who believed that they were being cheated were now further convinced of their theories and wasted no time in sharing their predictable views with captive audiences found in any crowded bar. And the speaker would begin 'Den yu no si what a happen?' And in the midst of the stunned silence they would continue with an air of disbelief 'Yu mean yu no see wha the man a do?' And hardly pausing for breath they continued with their theory of exploitation. 'Well, if you caan si what im a do den mi betta tell you. Im a get us fi buy his drink but im naa print any Y. Simple as dat! Dats how im a mek his money affa your back.' And as many of his audience looked on bemusedly with the drink created by robbers touching their parched lips, he would rage on without any encouragement 'Si! Ave we a drink like we mad an nat making any damn Y. Him just a rub im hand an a go to de bank. Yu si?' Then finally having had enough of his silent, unresponsive and probably inebriated audience, he (and similar cohorts across the island) would kiss his teeth and wander off, sipping at his last bottle while bemoaning his own bad luck and vowing, as he tossed his empty bottle into the undergrowth 'As God is my wickness, me naa go buy wana dem suppen again!' And back in the establishment, his audience, now totally chilled to the bone - but in a nice way, would return to sipping their ice-cold pacifier while they looked off into the distance and visualised taking ownership of not just the elusive letter but also of the promised magical steed.

And the frenzy of collecting was not just confined to adults but was also a hot topic amongst the school population, including the school attended by our friend Likkle wicked. And he, often while carrying out his playtime duties had listened nonchalantly as his friends spoke about the best shops from which to buy the soft drink and about ways of selecting a lucky bottle. Some children also spoke excitedly of people they knew who had had the most luck in collecting for their chosen items. And some even spoke quite freely of the best places for hiding treasured collections and told stories of people whose lives had been ruined because of voracious collecting and had had to borrow money to continue to achieve their dream. There were also harrowing tales of villagers who had amassed large stashes of the drink and yet had been unable to achieve the desired prize of a bicycle that would in turn have enabled them to repay their large loans, and so as a consequence, they had had to sell their treasured home. And other tales of people who had after social events away from home had returned to discover that their treasure had been pilfered; no doubt by someone with whom they had shared its secret location.

Sadly, during the fizzy drink frenzy, school came to an end for Likkle Wicked in an abrupt way. It was soon after receiving a reminder of the date of his impending exam on a hot afternoon, that he had become embroiled in an altercation with a teacher over a minor triviality, and not much later, the inevitable happened and he was seen being manhandled into the head teacher's study. Following some dull sounds - probable the result of cane making contact with khaki trousers - duly followed by loud cries and unexpected guttural exchanges, the office door was yanked open. And then out of the small room like a dog-track rabbit came our friend – a very angry Likkle Wicked, clutching in his fist the hated implement of torture which had been used to violently assault him. And as expected he was followed closely, but not closely enough as demonstrated by his outstretched arm, the headteacher, who while running, bellowed repeatedly 'stap right there bwoy!' While LW was of course silently encouraged in his desperate dash for freedom by his telepathic peers as he wended his way over obstacles like chairs, desks and even children, towards the exit. And as a finale, just before he took his final leap down the steep flight of steps, he gladdened the hearts of his supporters by breaking with a resounding snap, the feared cane with which many of his audience had already become reluctantly acquainted. Then still bellowing, he had like an unbridled horse, raced towards the picket fence which separated him from the great wide world. And thus, Likkle Wicked ended his tenure at Flaxman school.

***

Now, just like there was a desperate search for the letter Y amongst the pupils, so there had been the equally desperate search for information about the whereabouts of their long lost friend Likkle Wicked, following his escape from the iron grip of the headmaster. Finally, after several lines of enquiries had been issued, and mostly based on a recurring rumour, it was established as fact that he had been sent by his long-suffering grandmother – probably in a bid to escape being pushed over yet again – to live with his father in Kingston after he had returned from his cane-cutting job in Cuba.

Some months later on a cool Thursday afternoon, a group of children, selected as a reward for their good behaviour, were happily working with their head teacher on the task of weeding and watering the flowerbeds. And with bottle tops and the subject of the elusive letter Y still the main topic of conversation at all social gatherings, it was not surprising that one bold student enquired of the revered headteacher 'Sir do you collect bottle tops?

Understanding the fervour which had gripped the island the

head replied with a chuckle ‘No son, I don’t like the drink at all’. And following a short pause, he enquired ‘Are you collecting them?’

‘Yes, sir!’ the boy exclaimed while indicating by his tone that he had never before met anyone that did not. And the clamour of other voices expressed their surprise along with his; many adding how many they had, and even what prizes had so far been won by members of their families.

‘My mother won some pots sir.’

‘Oh, that is nice for her Denzel. Is she happy with them?’

‘Yes sir’, he said with obvious pride in his voice, before he continued ,’Sir, she’s so happy with them that she will not use them sir. She said she does not want to spoil them on the fire’.

And the lack of laughter indicated that that was the response of many parents up and down the land towards the items for which they had strived.

‘Is the same with my father and his dominos volunteered another boy. ‘He win a nice set but he won’t let anyone play with them. He just takes them out of the box and look at them in the evenings.’

But from the look on the faces of his audience including the headteacher, it could be discerned that the father’s attitude was not appreciated by all.

The headteacher, happy to be engaging with his pupils while they worked, picked up the conversation with the original questioner, and enquired as to what prize he himself hoped to win. And living amongst his community, if in a larger house, he of course was not surprised to learn of the boy’s wish for a bicycle and to hear of how the possession of one would improve his life and that of his family. And so the headteacher, bending under the sun with a small trowel in his hand and his own set of car keys quietly sitting in his pocket, did not feel justified to suggest that maybe the accumulation of all the money their hardworking families had spent on the brown liquid could have by now bought such a vehicle which held the power to change their lives in many ways.

It was while he had continued to listen to the clamour of their optimistic voices around him, their faces wreathed in dreams, that he had seen a sight from the corner of his eye that had made him gasp and straighten up. It was a sight he had never expected to see again. And the children, busy and deep in their animated talk and happy to have a willing listener, one by one, also paused and followed his astounded gaze. And they too gasped as they stared at the visitor who had by now come well within the boundaries of the school. One after the other they straightened up and watched their visitor as he travelled slowly down the gravelled drive towards them. And his manner was as nonchalant as it had always been. And they whispered his name with awe. Yes, it was none other than Likkle Wicked!

Now taller, broader, and to the smiling girls which included Cassie and her best friend Elaine, he was even more handsome than before. Even the boys noticed the change in him and fleetingly dreamed that in their later years – when they had truly become men – they too would have what he now sported – a beard! A close-cut one as worn by the male models seen in the numerous adverts for the soft brown drink. A tonsorial addition they decided that served to accentuate his trademark disarming smile and highlighted his teeth which at that moment appeared to be whiter and larger than they recalled. But the most astonishing feature of all that had impressed everyone, was the fact that he was moving, but not on his legs. On and on he came, slowly, with his upper body leaning forwards nonchalantly while the rest of him balanced at a precarious angle, on a shiny, brand new bicycle!

Then suddenly without a moment's thought as to the consequences of their actions, the mesmerised children abandoned their tools like useless articles and rushed headlong towards the returning boy and fell gratefully under his already raised and welcoming hand. In the melee some experienced a pat, while others felt the sweep of his hand across their low-cut hair. And during this anointing, the questions tumbled out and sought answers about him, about Kingston, about his previous whereabout, and most of all – about the bike. All questions rose into the air unanswered as still slowly moving, he smiled his film star smile above their heads, into the near distance.

And while they continued to repeat his name as if their tongue needed to convince their eyes that his presence was real and that in fact he wasn't a Duppy, they touched him in wonder, and gingerly stroked the smooth shiny metal of the slow-moving machine as they tried to satisfy their curiosity through their questions which rang out like a plaintive song.

'Likkle Wicked?' one said without any reason

'Licked Wicked?' another intoned like a chorus

'Where yu bin Likkle Wicked?' someone asked

'Likkle Wicked we missed you' said a low plaintive voice

'Whose bicycles is this Likkle Wicked? asked someone else

in a beseeching tone

And without reason, someone screeched 'Likkle Wicked!'

Then, 'Likkle Wicked, me can have ride?' a desperate voice implored.

'Please Likkle Wicked' someone begged outright

'Yu coming back to school Likkle Wicked?' a small but hopeful voice piped up

Then 'Likkle Wicked!' said a voice thirsty with adoration

And all the while, he Likkle Wicked looked on beyond their heads at the figure standing straight, regal and still, who looked straight back at his former student while the bud of a smile transformed itself into a full blown welcome. And the excited questioners paused in their exultation and their eyes travelled back and forth with amazement and delight towards the younger man and his elder. And as they watched, the greeting came

'How you doing Likkle Wicked my boy?'

And they the children wreathed in biblical teachings, looked on and felt the unspoken waves of forgiveness and pride which the older man conveyed without words above their heads, and towards their friend. And he the young man, the once recalcitrant student, the cane-breaker, reciprocated with the self-same emotions and with the additional component of respect towards the man who now strode towards him with open arms. And the hug was noted with joy and was celebrated wildly. Then the children, as is the nature of children when they are happy with the actions of adults, emulated what they had witnessed by grabbing, hugging, and in some cases, lifting each other from the ground while filling the air with whoops and cheers. And the moment was seared forever into their memory, and into the memory of the public who stood along the picket fence which separated the school from the highway.

But the fun had only just begun.

Buoyed up with love and myriad emotions, Likkle Wicked dismounted from his steed in one smooth movement, and the headteacher without hesitation, or any audible invitation or request, replaced Likkle Wicked in the saddle, and the audience, filled with amazement and unalloyed joy in every fibre of their bodies, and now beyond themselves with excitement, whooped and laughed with voices even louder than before. And many, to fully express their joy, leapt into the air while turning a full three hundred and sixty degrees as they cried out triumphantly 'Gwane Sir!' And a few, after their circular leap, had stood dumbfounded that their headteacher, the driver of the long American car, also had the skill to sit upright on a bicycle. And thinking back to their earlier conversation before Likkle Wicked had made his entrance, they now wondered with their child-like simplicity why had he also had not been collecting tokens. And so, as it is with children, they waited patiently for proof of his skills.

'How im know to ride?'

'Me neva know im can ride!'

'Me tort him can only drive.'

And one child eager to prove themself knowledgeable, interjected in a know-it-all manner displayed by bookish children with a hint of disdain 'Of course, im can drive and ride. Im have hand and foot don't he?

But this did not stop the disbelief of some who needed

practical proof.

'Shush!' they said, sensing a rebuke, 'Mek us watch no!'

So, they watched their headteacher sitting in the saddle and looking as comfortable and almost as stylish as Likkle Wicked had. And they also observed how upright and motionless he remained while firmly gripping the shiny black leather wraps of the handlebars which curved around towards him like the horns of a thoroughbred bull; and how in a testing sort of manner he gently pumped the brakes which lay beneath them. And they also saw how he surveyed the large bulbous bell, and then with his head slightly cocked to one side, how he twanged the protuberance and smiled broadly at his audience as the shrill sound rang out. And in return, they laughed uproariously while replicating – as children will – his thumb movements and they repeatedly copied the sound which the bell had produced; actions which of course generated further laughter.

Then finally, with his feet comfortably ensconced in the stirrups, and after clamorous call to 'Go on sir!' and, 'ride it sir' 'ride it!' 'ride it!' he gave a slight nod to Likkle Wicked who stood nonchalantly by with his hands deep into his pockets. And then with a look of pure joy liberally displayed across his lightly tanned face, the rider now leaned forward in the saddle as if charging into an everlastingly mighty gale, and set his long legs working. Slowly at first, then faster and faster like pistons, he picked up speed and left his sauntering followers in his wake as the magnificent machine like a winged chariot carried him off at breakneck speed around the schoolhouse. Then as he belted along the perimeter of the long building, the breeze he had created, entered the space between his crisp white shirt and his body underneath, and instantly added hundreds of pounds to the normally svelte shape of the rider. And the children, once more beside themselves with happiness, hollered with delight and flew along behind him, desperate to witness his lap of honour.

Finally, the headteacher, smiling from ear to ear and so almost unrecognisable, dismounted his steed to great applause and jubilation. And then it was the turn of Likkle Wicked. Sensing that expectations were high, he mounted his two wheeled chariot and just for effect, carried out safety checks which included the bell ringing procedure which once again had the audience in stitches. Then pedalling furiously up a steep incline towards the enormous Poinsettia tree, he paused briefly, turned with legs splayed out as far away from the pedals as he could, and manoeuvred the bicycle at great speed down the incline as if on course to collide with the admiring group; and they, fully enjoying the added drama, dived dramatically and in the nick of time, out of harm's way. Actually, just as Likkle Wicked wildly peeling his bell and picking up speed, rose the front portion of his steed up into the air before suddenly bringing it back down to earth while simultaneously applying his brakes hard and apparently with no danger of him flying over the handlebars. The applause following this act of bravado was deafening. And in return he flashed his trademark smile,

Then following refreshment and with the sun travelling speedily towards the horizon, the time for farewell had arrived. And as the hand of the older man met the younger in a symbol of friendship and goodbye, the headteacher, forever the moral compass of the community said, while bearing a discernible twinkle in his eyes, 'Son, when yu have some time you must come back to one of our assemblies and tell us the story of how you got your Y'. And he had noted that for a fleeting instance, a wry smile had alighted on the face of the young man as he had answered in a clear and sincere voice, 'Yes sir'. 'I will sir'. And then, just before he turned to go, he said the words which to the children were inexplicable. He said, 'I'm very sorry sir'.

And a look of understanding and pure love passed between them and something, one eagle-eyed boy observed, was pressed into the hand of the young man. Then Mr. Wilson had stood and watched his former pupil progress stylishly down the drive and out through the gate, followed closely by his cavalcade of noisy admirers screaming their goodbyes and taking the opportunity to have a last touch of his clothes – and of his gleaming mud guards.

Then having entered the Content Road, one lone boy who had outran the others was heard to scream desperately 'How did you get your Y Likkle Wicked? And the answer it was said had returned on the wind 'Me jus lucky, man. Me jus lucky.'

And it was only after his visit, that news came in thick and fast, of other lucky winners. But everyone in the district and beyond knew that Likkle Wicked had been the first to find a Y.

The Potion

Not only did the large white van bring to the very heart of the community the whole Jamaican Top Ten hit parade, but it also brought something for which many of the population thirsted – a large consignment of Andrews Liver Salt. Something which in the absence of a nearby or affordable doctor, they kept as an insurance against any ailment that might beset any member of their family or community.

And this cure-all was the item which Cassie had hurriedly purchased soon after Boysie had said his goodbyes and driven off into the darkness. And indeed, many of those who had been in the crowd dancing and cavorting might have on their arrival home found that the pick me up that they now desperately needed was none other than the refreshing flavour of Andrews Liver Salts, even though the person looking back at them in the mirror was blooming with health and vivacity and vigour.

However, regarding the potion, any excuses would do in a bid to sample its invigorating fizz. Because it was due to reports of its restorative powers from personages up and down the land over the decades, that the innocent-looking white powder had been elevated into the echelons of indispensability and had therefore become a permanent fixture in every home. And beyond the name so elegantly inscribed on each tin, nothing else strived to illuminate and explain the contents of what lay inside. So powerful was its history and its fame that the makers did not deem it necessary to utilise the remaining surfaces of the cylindrical tin with any further information. So there was no mention of contents or method of preparation, list of ingredients or indeed any reviews or recommendations from previous customers. That information its makers felt would be superfluous and could never convey – if indeed it was necessary to do so – the esteemed qualities of their magical powder.

And neither was there any explanation of who 'Andrews' was. Or whether the name was a surname or Christian name, or who had donated the liver, or indeed the process whereby said liver had been converted into the powdery contents as well as the process by which the liver had been miraculously converted from red to white. Instead, what the avid consumers had learned over the years was that the compound held by them in such high regard was imbued with magical powers and could work wonders on the digestive system of the entire population of the country.

And over the years many people had had cause to reflect on the many times and in the various locations that they had been present at its dispensation, or indeed had been the recipient of its life-giving qualities. And it was on these occasions whether as willing patient, keen dispenser or curious onlooker that they had observed the sacred never-varying ritual of its delivery to the sick, injured, or even those it had been said, were on the very edge of death.

Because its consumption was reserved for the sick, many robust malingers too lazy it was said to conjure up a valid reason for wanting to sample its properties, were willing to simply appear listless and in poor health, in a bid to sample the delights of the potion. And many in this group were usually given short shrift after being keenly assessed by members of the Andrews Liver Salts Experts sorority who had been named by a prolific creator of nicknames as ALSE. Their unquestionable verdicts once cast down, would swiftly dispatch villains by way of stern admonishment to 'Go wey and stap a try to waste me precious Andrews liva salts'. Followed by exhortations to 'Go wey and fine something betta to do dan waste people time and money'. And the final words hurled at the back of the swiftly departing villain confirming that they had been rumbled in their dishonesty was 'Bout yu sick! Yu look more hail an harty dan me. Go wey!', before a final high-pitched kissing of the teeth which always indicated that the matter was closed to any form of begging.

The magical powder not only held a pride of place in the hearts of the populace but was held in a secure hiding place within every home. And this place was privy to every member of the family young or old; and even if their physical stature prevented them from prizing it from such a place in time of need, they could if asked, accurately pinpoint its position even with their eyes closed. And if their knowledge of preparation was ever questioned, they would have without any hesitation been able to dispense and even perform the legendary ceremonies that were necessary to produce the cure for any perceived ailment.

And the rules for receiving the curative powder followed a strict and unwavering order. First the patient is ordered to sit, while the dispenser of the hallowed powder, bearing a look on their stern visage, which suggest to the patient and any curious onlookers, that the administrator had been chosen by destiny and specially imbued with the power of administering this elixir. All would watch as that hallowed personage would retrieve the curative from its hallowed hiding place before regally but purposefully moving towards the patient and employing steps which suggested that they were treading on hallowed ground and honouring their destiny. Then standing above the waiting and wilting supplicant, with the cylindrical tin clutched firmly in one hand and a large deep-scooped spoon and a glass precisely half filled with what appeared to the naked eye to be just ordinary, and clear – but pure – tap water, they would seat themselves beside the once deeply watchful person who had quickly transformed themselves into a willing patient.

Then while the now very sick one looked on with rapidly drooping features which suggested that death was at the door peeping in, the lid of the sacred tin would be gently yet urgently prized upwards at various juncture of its circular configuration with the end of the deep-scooped spoon, until finally it was silently released from its deep-set recesses. Then with the release operation complete, a heaped spoonful of the glistening white powder, no more no less - as calculated with instinct and the eye, rather than mathematical precision – would be displayed in mid-air for just a few seconds for the purpose of allowing the audience and patient to momentarily admire its white sparkling beauty. And on every occasion, it would be observed by the onlookers that during this fleeting period of beholding, the eyes of the sick one would appear to emit what looked like sparks of ever-increasing hope, where before there had been only despair and utter resignation to their fate. Some even went as far as to say they had heard a distant choir.

Then suddenly and without warning or further prevarications, the dispenser would dramatically plunge the contents of the heaped spoon deep through the surface of the water and right down to the very bottom of the receptacle. And just as suddenly, from the depths of that receptacle there came like a once resting monster aroused from its slumber, a sudden commotion which quickly and magically transformed itself into a torrential explosion of bubbles of the wildest and most extraordinary consistency of frothiness of which any sorcerer would have been justly proud. This creation, this tornado, would as from a boiling cauldron rise up uncontrollably into a foaming, popping and volcanic edifice of magic which threatened at every! Pop! Pop! Pop! to rise beyond the confines of the glass as it raged to more than double its effervescence and seemed intent on rising to the ceiling.

But this cataclysmic eruption, everyone including the recipient knew, could only achieve its latent promise if the patient fully played his or her part. And their part, as had silently been agreed before the whole procedure began, was not to shrink from the edifice of bubbles and noisiness, but to engage with it in its entirety and proceed to consume it all and prevent its ascent to the ceiling. But not at a leisurely pace. Oh no! Instead, they had to muster every bit of their flagging energy and meet the tornado with gusto, with relish, and with a greed and urgency which matched the dramatic profusion of the volcanic eruptions.

And so, the theatre would begin with the patient's gulpings. Gulpings that were so desperate and gravalicious in nature, that it suggested to the dispenser and onlookers alike, that the gulper's life depended on it. That it was their duty to ensure that not even a small drop was wasted as they valiantly gulped in the noisiest and most greedy fashion. And to everyone present it would seem also as if they strived to win a race with no discernible finishing post, one in which they had not willingly in their sick state agreed to participate. Yes, one in which the rule was to consume a tumbler full of raging white water before the bubbles subsided and lost their potency. A race which during its course seemed to consume the last vestiges of energy that the patient possessed – before the magic of the powder and its effervescent bubbles and curative powers subsided and were forever lost and thus, in the administrator's view, wasted.

And while this desperate race against time was enacted, the onlookers played their part as hecklers who constantly and noisily jockeyed the patient on to the finishing line and so prevented them from throwing in the towel of drinking or giving up in the struggle for recovery. And this vocal rooting for success would begin at the initial delivery of the potion.

'Open yu moute!' they would cry as soon as the liquid exploded upwards in a torrent of bubbles, and indeed even before the patient's lips had made contact with the receptacle. And the sick one already at death's door would seem to visibly muster up the energy and indeed courage to begin their gulpings. Now they would be driven on with wilder exhortations of 'Open yu mouth wydah! Wydah! Then as if the drinker could do anything but drink, they would add 'Drink it! 'drink it! And the room would immediately resonate with the sound of urgent 'Gulp! gulp! gulp!' Then the dispenser with rising alarm in her voice as she watched the subsidence of the bubbles through the walls of the glass , would screech in alarm 'Yu wasting it... Drink it!' this last uttered with the urgency of a punter urging his horse to the finishing line. And the exhausted but keen drinker, acknowledging the need for urgency, would oblige with even more desperate eye-rolling gulps as if his or her life truly depended on it; and so quite audible sounds of the gullet working to its maximum ability would begin to fill the sick room. And in addition to this desperate struggle, there was also a keen vigilance on the part of the administrator for any wastage that might be making tracks along the edges of the patient's mouth; and if noted there would be a cry which suggested that the patient was in mortal danger, with the words 'Look! It a drip out!' followed by the urgent instruction of 'Me say drink it! Drink it!'

And so, it was towards the conclusion of the race that the gullet signalled itself to being almost on the verge of collapse as the patient gulped with a desperation that seemed to cause as well as a bulging oesophagus, eyes that seemed to be on the verge of expulsion from their reddened sockets too. And to prevent any slacking at this point of the operation , the vigilant administrator would keep up the momentum of rapidly repeated instructions of 'Don't stap, don't stap! Then 'Drink de last drap!' and again as before 'A say drink it! drink it!' this final instruction, released from the patient, now depleted of all energy, a final exhausted and hardly audible 'Gulp!'

Then finally to indicate the end of the ordeal, 'Awright, awright. Stap now! Stap now!' is screeched by the very vigilant self-appointed nurse, before the empty glass is held upside down and brandished under the nose with the final words of 'Si! Notting no lef in it'. And at this stage, bystanders too would take the opportunity to closely scrutinise the receptacle from all angles, and so were also able to see that no residue of the precious powder remained outside of the body of the now exhausted patient. Following this display, events would move swiftly to the second and final phase.

It usually began with a murmur of unquestionable success from the director of the whole event before she (and it was always she) proceeded to brusquely rouse the cured patient from their prone and ambient position while indicating by the finality in her voice that (if addressing a child) they should run along and get on with whatever task, duty or journey they were previously engaged in before they registered themselves as being in need of the curative powder. But in the case of adult patients, their cure had to pass through another stage before being given the all-clear. And to gain that status, they must fully comply with all request in a bid to provide the physical evidence which would attest to them having once more reached the pinnacle of robust health. And based on former knowledge gained either as a patient or as a spectator, only they and no one else is able to provide the administrator and onlookers with that necessary evidence. They alone must provide the proof that they were worthwhile beneficiaries and imbibers of the magical powder, since they alone drank the potion.

What you may ask, is further required of them after almost being drowned through the process of drinking the volcanic liquid? Well dear eader, not only must the patient be seen to have benefited from the precious curative, but the audience and administrator must also derive some benefits for their acts of mercy towards their now cured patient. So, the patient now sitting upright, must give proof to show that their imbibing had had a truly beneficial and curative effect on their constitution. But this cannot simply be through an everyday gesture of 'Thanks'. To the audience that is no proof. Instead, it has to be through a physical manifestation, louder and more dramatic than mere words. And from the slightly hunted look in the patient's eyes, they already know this. They know that they will only be released from their obligation through an exhibition which is in some cultures seen as the height of bad manners. But not here in Jamaica. For following the ingesting of the rare medication, they know that it is obligatory for the patient to produce that specific kind of evidence and gratitude. And that obligation can only be suitably delivered through what can only be described as 'The Belch'. This to the uninitiated is the rigorous oral expulsion of a conglomeration of bubbles otherwise known as 'gas', which after invading the body can only be expelled though the mouth after difficult contortions.

The patient knows that a puny sputtering of bubbles emanating from the regions of his or her oesophagus and without tumultuous noise or discomfort will not suffice. No, the audience and administration have higher expectations, and will require instead the blood curdling and roaring sound of wind emanating from every cell within their newly revived body. Yes, what they want is a resounding belch of stupendous quality emanating from every pore and sinew, and finally emanating from the patients gaping mouth with further horrific bulging of the eyeballs. And they also know that the final results is one that the poor by now exhausted patient has striven desperately for. One in fact that causes great monster-like contortions of the face and neck sinews and for which they have suffered manfully to achieve. Then and only then, on the production of such a belch, can a full recovery be deemed to have taken place.

And for the administrator that does not mean a polite hands-over-mouth, eyelash-fluttering, coy, apologetic variety of explosion described as a burp'; no, that will not be sufficient. To be deemed authentic it must be full-throttled and its depth and volume must extend and echo beyond the confines of the room in which patient, audience and dispenser reside. And only on delivery of that truly cataclysmic expulsion of air, or gas, will the whole exercise be deemed as having been worthwhile thus proving to all, near and as far away as possible, that the dispensation of the precious powder and exact quantity of water had not been wasted on an undeserving patient feigning a malady.

So now, the recovering one, well-versed in how this

cataclysmic explosion can be achieved, proceeds to create one in the age-old fashion of vigorous squeezing and stroking of their ribcage while simultaneously opening and closing their mouths in a gasping motion akin to that of a fish literally out of water and in the last throes of death. Now with the continued pummelling of the thoracic region, the audience, now convinced that the required results are nigh, begins to encourage the process on by vocalising their sympathy with the beleaguered one by unconsciously and in a spirit of brotherhood, gasping like fishes and stroking their torso in unison with the patient – all the while nodding as they murmur litanies for the desperate one.

And then not a moment too soon, there is a pause as the patient's eyes, bulging and almost totally expulsed from their sockets – produces from the depths of their tortured and writhing torso, an orchestra of sounds and rhythms which could easily be mistaken for a loud and undisciplined band of drummers, as the evidence of gas registers itself then begins to make its vigorous and undeterred way through the highways, byways and alleyways of the chest regions.

Now as it enters the neck region there can plainly be heard what could be described as a distant rock fall as the collected conglomeration struggles to escape into the atmosphere through the narrow aperture of the neck region, and in the process causes the patient to visibly tremble as though in the final throes of expiring. And just before the patient begins to mouth a final prayer, the whole tornado erupts upwards and into the patient's now wide, stiffly gaping and quivering mouth and sends out a tumultuous, rip roaring, animal-scaring, prolonged, and bone-trembling explosion. It is the sound for which they, most of all the exhausted patient has been waiting for. Like a true fanfare, it issues forth into the confines of the room, disturbing the previously still curtains before it proceeds into the street to startle passers-by and maybe even sleeping dogs who, alerted by what they believe to be the tremors of an earthquake, rises swiftly on unsteady legs and barks loudly at an invisible enemy.

And then finally as peace returns to the confines of the room there can be seen on the face of the caregiver, a broad smile of satisfaction as she saunters confidently, tin in hand, towards the sacred hiding place of her precious Andrews Liver Salts.

And sometimes, there will even be the sound of whistling before the patient is once more released in the wild.

Other titles by Author...

Coming soon...

A Jamaican Childhood Book 3

A Jamaican Dawn Drawing Book

Windrush Child: Arriving in England

The Exodus and Arrival
Windrush Activity book

For further information please email author at:
ajamaicanchildhood@gmail.com

Printed in Great Britain
by Amazon